Arcola Theatre and CASA Latin
presents

Thebes
by **Sergio Blanco**

a
theatre

Cast	**Trevor White**
	Alex Austin

Direction & Adaptation	**Daniel Goldman**
Literal Translation	**Rob Cavazos**
Design	**Jemima Robinson**
Lighting and Video Design	**Richard Williamson**
Sound Design	**Elena Peña**
Production Manager	**Bryan Novelo**
	for eStage Production
Stage Manager	**Anna Sheard**
Associate Director	**Gianluca Lello**
Photogaphy	**Alex Brenner**
Assistant Director	**Mariana Aritstizábal Pardo**
Assistant Director (Revival)	**Gemma Aked-Priestley**
Assistant Designer	**Malena Arcucci**

This production first performed Wednesday 30 November 2016
at Arcola Theatre, London

Supported by Arts Council England Grants for the Arts
and the Royal Victoria Hall Foundation

RVH
ROYAL VICTORIA HALL
FOUNDATION

Supported using public funding by
ARTS COUNCIL
ENGLAND

The Company

Trevor White
S

Theatre includes: *Long Day's Journey Into Night* (West End); *Enron* (West End/ Royal Court/Chichester); *Henry IV Pt. I & II, Coriolanus* (RSC); *The Machine* (Donmar Warehouse/NY); *Red Bud, Aunt Dan, Lemon* (Royal Court); *On the Record* (Arcola); *Macbeth* (Regent's Park); *Purple Heart* (Gate); *Terrorism* (Bush).
Film includes: *The Dark Knight Rises, Jason Bourne, World War Z, Mad To Be Normal, A Summer In Genova, Burton & Taylor, The Whistleblower, Mindhunters, Die Another Day, Hellraiser: Hellseeker.* Upcoming: *American Assassin, Anchor A Hope, Astral.* Television includes: *Downton Abbey, Episodes, Hunted, X Company, Foyle's War, Moonshot, House of Saddam, The Path to 9/11, The Line of Beauty, SS-GB.* Upcoming: *The Durrells, Series 2.*
Radio includes: *Tales of The City, Homefront, The Assassination of JFK, Double Indemnity, The Clintons, The Octoroon, Hombre, The 33, Moby Dick, The Great Gatsby, Revolutionary Road.*

Alex Austin
Martin Santos / Freddie

Theatre includes: *Primetime, Fury* (Soho Theatre); *Yen, Pigeons* (Royal Court); *Barbarians* (Young Vic); *Skriker* (Royal Exchange Manchester); *Henry V, Nutcracker, The Man with the Incredibly Smelly Foot, How to think the Unthinkable* (Unicorn); *Idomeneus* (Gate); *My City* (Almeida); *Encourage the Others, Telling Tales* (Almeida Young Company).
Television includes: *Liar, Humans 2, Sherlock, The Interceptor, The Musketeers, New Tricks, Holby City, Misfits.*
Film includes: *A Moving Image, The Hooligan Factory, Legacy, The World's End, Christmas Candle, The Sweeney, Undefeated.*
Radio includes: *Tales Of The City, The Life And Loves Of A She Devil, Homefront, Moby Dick, Hombre, The 33, Tender Is The Night, The Long Goodbye, The Great Gatsby and Revolutionary Road.* Upcoming: *Playing With Fire, The Truth About Anna.*

Sergio Blanco
Text

Sergio is a Franco-Uruguayan playwright and stage director. He spent his childhood and adolescence in Montevideo and currently lives in Paris. His work – which has been translated, published and performed in several countries – has been awarded the National Playwriting Award of Uruguay, the Playwriting Award of the Municipality of Montevideo, the Prize of the National Fund Theatre, the Florencio Award for Best Playwright, the International Casa de las Americas prize and The Theatre Awards for the best Text in Greece. His plays *.45'* and *Kiev* entered the repertoire of the National Comedy Uruguay in 2003 and 2007. **His other works include:** *Slaughter, Opus Sextum, Diptiko (vol 1 and 2)*; *Barbarie, Kassandra, El Salto de Darwin, Ostia, La Ira de Narciso* and *El Bramido Düsseldorf.*

Daniel Goldman
Direction & Adaptation

Daniel is the artistic director of Tangram Theatre Company (www.tangramtheatre. co.uk) and CASA Latin American Theatre Festival (www.casafestival.org. uk). **Shows include:** *4.48 Psychosis* (ORL/Arcola); *Crunch!* (Edinburgh Fringe/ UK & International touring); *Fucked* (ORL/Edinburgh Fringe); *Richard III, Fuente Ovejuna, The Dragon* (Southwark Playhouse); *Wanawake Waheri Wa Windsa* (Shakespeare's Globe/ International Touring); *The Origin of Species..., Albert Einstein: Relativitively Speaking, The Element in the Room* (Edinburgh Fringe/ UK & International Touring); *Team Viking, A hundred different words for love* (Vault Festival/Edinburgh Fringe/UK Touring). **Awards include:** The Better Bankside Shakespeare Award, The Stage Award for Solo Performance, two Off West End Awards for Best Production and Best Children's Show, the Adelaide Critics Award, a Three Weeks Editors Award and Three Vault Festival Awards (including Best Show of the Year). **Award nominations include:** an Olivier Award, a Total Theatre Award, the Jerwood Award and the JMK award. Daniel has also worked across the globe directing shows in English, French, Hindi, Spanish and Swahili and regularly works as a director/actor trainer in leading UK and international drama schools.

Jemima Robinson
Design

Jemima is the winner of the biennial Linbury Prize for Stage Design and the Bristol Old Vic Technical Theatre Award in 2011. She is a former resident artist at Kenya's Kuona Arts Trust in Nairobi and resident designer for Istanbul's Talimhane Theatre. Jemima was awarded the Max Rayne Design Bursary at the National Theatre is currently their resident design assistant.

Her recent UK Design credits include: *The Majority* (National Theatre); *Mapping Brent* (Tricycle theatre); *New Nigerians, Thebes Land* (Nominated for Best Set Design: Offie Award); *Maria de Buenos Aires* (Arcola) *Parallel Yerma* (Young Vic); *License To Ill, This Will End Badly* (Southwark Playhouse); *Biedermann and the arsonists* (Sadlers Wells); *DYL, Sparks* (Old Red Lion); *Hearing Things* (Albany).

Richard Williamson
Lighting & Video Design

Richard trained at LAMDA. **Previous work includes:** *New Nigerians, Drones Baby Drones* (also video); *Shrapnel* (also video); *Mare Rider, Boy With a Suitcase, Peer Gynt, Macbeth, A Midsummer Night's Dream, The Night Just Before the Forest, Tartuffe, Through a Cloud, King Arthur, Mojo Mickybo, The Great Theatre of the World, Tombstone Tales, The Country* (Arcola);*Richard III, An Arab Tragedy* (Swan Theatre Stratford/International tour); *Septimus Bean and His Amazing Machine, Jason and the Argonauts* (Unicorn); *The Body* (Barbican); *The Easter Rising and Thereafter* (Jermyn Street); *Rotterdam* (Theatre 503/Trafalgar Studios); *The Dark Side of Love* (Roundhouse); *In My Name, Boris World King* (Trafalgar Studios); *Amphibians* (Bridewell); *Thrill Me* (Tristan Bates/Charing Cross Theatre/UK tour); *The Last Session* (Tristan Bates); *Twentieth Century Boy* (New Wolsey Ispwich); *Re:Home* (also video); *Brenda* (The Yard); *Play Size* (Young Vic); *The Al-Hamlet Summit* (Tokyo International Festival/International tour); *Strangers In Between, Ballo, Tosco, Denial, Someone To Blame* (Kings Head); *Summer Begins* (Southwark Playhouse). Richard is Head of Production for C venues at the Edinburgh Festival, and is a Trustee of the Kings Head Theatre. www.richard-williamson.com

Elena Peña
Sound Design

Theatre includes: *The Caretaker* (Bristol Old Vic); *Wondr* (Metta); *HIR* (Bush); *The Bear and The Proposal* (Young Vic); *I Call My Brothers, The Iphigenia Quartet, The Christians, Unbroken* (Gate); *The Lounge* (Soho); *Man Who Would Be King* (Dawn State); *Sleepless* (Analogue, Staatstheater, Mainz, Germany); *Patrias, Quimeras* (Sadler's Wells); *Arabian Nights, The Kilburn Passion* (Tricycle); *Brainstorm* (National Theatre); *Soechon Odyssey* (Hi Seoul Festival, Korea); *Not Now Bernard, Pim & Theo* (Unicorn); *A High Street Odyssey* (NT Watch This Space Festival); *Flashes* (Young Vic); *Mass Observation* (Almeida); *Gambling* (Soho Theatre);

The 13 Midnight Challenges of Angelus Diablo (RSC); *Under Milk Wood* (Northampton Theatre Royal).
Sound installation includes: *Yes, These Eyes Are The Windows and Have Your Circumstances Changed* (ArtAngel). **Radio includes:** *12 Years, The Meet Cute and Duchamps Urinal*.
Television includes: *Live from Television Centre: Brainstorm*.

Anna Sheard
Stage Manager

Anna trained at the Royal Welsh College of Music and Drama.
As Stage Manager credits include: *Pixel Dust/Wondr* (Metta); *Assata Taught Me, I Call My Brothers* (Gate); *Upper Cut* (W14 Productions, Southwark Playhouse); *Sweet Charity* (NYMT, Leicester Curve); *Danny the Champion of the World* (London Contemporary Theatre, UK Tour); *Lizzie Siddal* (Arcola).
As Deputy Stage Manager credits include: *House/ Amongst the Reeds* (Clean Break, Yard Theatre); *The Buskers Opera* (Park); *Lotty's War* (Yvonne Arnaud, UK Tour); *An Incident at the Border* (Finborough/Trafalgar Studios 2).
As Assistant Stage Manager credits include: *The Importance of Being Earnest* (Royal Opera House, Barbican); *Alice's Adventures in Wonderland* (Opera Holland Park); *Dancing at Lughnasa* (Theatre by the Lake); *Spamalot* (ATG, Playhouse Theatre); *Farragut North* (Southwark Playhouse).

Gianluca Lello
Associate Director

Gianluca is a recent graduate from The Liverpool Institute for Performing Arts, where he was awarded the Anthony Field Prize for Producing. He is currently working as the Co-Director of CASA Latin American Theatre Festival's 2017 Play Reading Festival. Previous work for the Arcola includes assisting during the development of new musical *The Queen and I*. Gianluca is also one of the Producers of short film production company Morphine Productions.

Mariana Aristizábal Pardo
Assistant Director

Mariana is the recipient of a CASA Emerging Latin American Artist bursary. She trained at The Royal Central School of Speech and Drama and at the Universidad Distrital in Bogotá, Colombia. Mariana has worked both as a solo performer-creator and has devised collaborative performances in interdisciplinary projects that involve theatre, dance and music. Parallel to this she has worked as a translator and teacher. Mariana's work explores her personal experience as a social and political body. **Recent works include:** *Cansancio Tears* (Brink Festival, Unscene Festival); *New girl in the room* (Short film); *Emperatriz del Viento y Reina de Nada* (Beca Unipersonal IDARTES). In collaboration with Malena Arcucci, Mariana is currently developing *I Occur Here* for CASA Latin American Theatre Festival 2017 to be presented at Southwark Playhouse in October.

Germma Aked-Priestley
Assistant Director (Revival)

Gemma is a freelance director and studied Theatre Directing at Mountview Academy of Theatre Arts. **Directing credits include:** *Rat King* (The Bunker); *Cold Call* (Theatre 503); *Biscuit* (Tristan Bates); *Grimm: An Untold Tale* (Underbelly, Edinburgh Fringe). **Assistant directing credits include:** *Tonight with Donny Stixx* (The Bunker); *Lockhart* (Bernie Grant Arts Centre). Gemma is also the assistant director for The Mono Box, a collaborative, not-for- profit network that caters for actors and theatre-makers seeking alternative, affordable training. Currently, she is developing *Passing* by Indigo Griffiths, a new play exploring the underground world of racial passing.

Malena Arcucci
Design Assistant

Malena studied in Buenos Aires, Granada and London. Malena is the recipient of a CASA Emerging Latin American Artist bursary. **Credits include:** *Orlando and the Three Graces, Clown* (Theatre Peckham); The Fall (Empatheyes Theatre Company); *Romeo and Juliet* (Centro Cultural Recoleta); *Casa Adentro* (Teatro del Pueblo); *Somos Tierra* (Argentinian tour); *Los 5 Sentidos Capitales* (Teatro de la Carbonera). In collaboration with Mariana Aristizábal, Malena is currently developing *I Occur Here* for CASA Latin American Theatre Festival 2017 to be presented at Southwark Playhouse in October.

arcola theatre

Arcola is one of London's leading off-West End theatres.

Locally engaged and internationally minded, Arcola stages a diverse programme of plays, operas and musicals. World-class productions from major artists appear alongside cutting-edge work from the most exciting emerging companies. Arcola delivers one of London's most extensive community engagement programmes, creating over 5000 opportunities every year. By providing research and development space to diverse artists, Arcola champions theatre that's more engaging and representative. Its pioneering environmental initiatives are internationally renowned, and aim to make Arcola the world's first carbon-neutral theatre.

MAKE THIS HAPPEN Become a Supporter from just £4.17 a month
www.arcolatheatre.com/support

www.arcolatheatre.com   Bloomberg **H Hackney**   ARTS COUNCIL ENGLAND

CASA LATIN AMERICAN THEATRE FESTIVAL

CASA Latin American Theatre Festival was founded in 2007 by Daniel Goldman to present the very best of Latin American theatre to UK audiences. Over the past nine years, it has become an internationally-renowned festival that has presented the work of over 100 Latin American artists to UK audiences, supported over 200 UK-based Latin American artists and actively engaged over 500 of London's Latin American community as participants in theatre activities.

CASA has won two Best Arts Festival LUKAS awards in 2013 and 2014 and been nominated for the same award in 2012 and 2015. Shows supported by CASA have gone on to tour the UK and Latin America and win a Fringe First and a Three Week Editor's Award.

Thebes Land CASA
Production Team:
Daniel Goldman
Cordelia Grierson
Catalina Herrera Acuna
Andrea S. Ortiz
Fernanda Aguirre
Sarah Ruff
Felix Andrew

CASA Latin American Theatre Festival Trustees:
Oliver Carruthers
Andy Wood
Fernardo Abadie
Andre Piza

Thanks:
Anonymous
Anne Richards
Cassandra Fumi
Cassandra Mathers
Jacquie Rosenbach
Mark Astaire
Paco de la Coba
Stephen and Nicole Goldman
The Royal Victoria Foundation

Thanks also to our partners:
Arts Council England
El Iberico
Queen Mary's University London
La Tundra

Finally, a special thank you to Lora Krasteva for her tireless dedication to CASA over the past five years.

www.casafestival.org.uk
info@casafestival.org.uk
@casafestival
/CasaLatinAmericanTheatreFestival

CASA Theatre Festival Ltd. Company Registered in England Number: 07284541 Registered Charity Number: 1152644 Registered Office Address: 1 The Causeway, Sutton, Surrey, SM2 5RS

THEBES LAND

Sergio Blanco

THEBES LAND

Translated and adapted by Daniel Goldman

Based on a literal translation by Roberto Cavazos

OBERON BOOKS
LONDON

WWW.OBERONBOOKS.COM

First published in 2016 by Oberon Books Ltd
521 Caledonian Road, London N7 9RH
Tel: +44 (0) 20 7607 3637 / Fax: +44 (0) 20 7607 3629
e-mail: info@oberonbooks.com
www.oberonbooks.com

A catalogue record for this book is available from the British
Library.

PB ISBN: 9781786820938
E ISBN: 9781786820945

Cover image by Alex Brenner

Printed and bound by 4edge Limited, Essex, UK.
eBook conversion by CPI Group (UK) Ltd, Croydon, CR0 4YY.

Visit www.oberonbooks.com to read more about all our books
and to buy them. You will also find features, author interviews and
news of any author events, and you can sign up for e-newsletters
so that you're always first to hear about our new releases.

Foreword One

If you're reading this foreword BEFORE watching the play I heartily recommend you close this book now and only open it after you've seen the show. Of course, what you actually do is your choice.

Welcome to *Thebes Land*.

* * *

Foreword Two

If you're yet to see the show and you've ignored or simply haven't seen the suggestion on the previous page that you stop reading this book, please resist the temptation to keep on reading now. Close this text. It's very easy to do. I promise you'll enjoy the show much more if you don't know what is about to happen. Again, this, of course, is only a recommendation. You may wish to know what happens next. It's a natural urge. Even Oedipus kept on looking when he could have looked away and far more important people than me told him to stop looking. And we all know what happened to Oedipus's eyes.

* * *

You see right through the heart of me,
You break down my walls.

I Have Nothing
Whitney Houston

* * *

Piano Concerto N° 21 in C major
Wolfgang Amadeus Mozart

* * *

You've got the blood on your hands
I think it's my own

Blue Blood
Foals

* * *

True poetry is outside laws

The Impossible
George Bataille

* * *

FIBA OFFICIAL BASKETBALL RULES

Rule 4.4.2.

Players shall not wear equipment (objects) that may cause injury to other players. It is forbidden to wear watches, rings, chains, bracelets or any other item that could cut or cause abrasions to a fellow player. Any player wearing a dangerous item will be ejected from the court of play and will not be able to return for the duration of the game.

* * *

The fork was introduced in Europe at the beginning of the 11th century by Teodora, daughter of the Emperor of Constantinople, Constantine X of the Ducas Dynasty. Teodora brought the fork alongside other Byzantine artefacts to the Venetian court as part of her dowry to the Doge Domenico Selvo. For said gifts, she was mocked and ridiculed with a leading figure of the church, San Pedro Damian, denouncing from the pulpit that the fork was the devil's instrument.

* * *

Characters

S, playwright, late thirties, early forties

MARTIN SANTOS, patricide, twenty-one

FREDDIE, actor, twenty-one

FIRST QUARTER

S: Are we all good to start? Great. Well. Hello and good
   evening everybody. I hope you're all comfortable? Yes.
   Good. So. Welcome. I'm going to try and explain in as few
   words as possible the context of what we're about to do
   here. So. About five years ago, I was standing right here
   in this very theatre, performing in a show called *On The
   Record* about press censorship, (which some of you may
   have seen). It was a great play, really political, and I loved
   being here, and at some point I was sitting in the bar after
   the show, and I told Mehmet Ergen, who runs the Arcola
   (for those of you that didn't already know that) I had a
   couple of ideas for plays I was working on, and he asked
   me to send them to him and I did. Mehmet read over
   the the ideas and liked them, and we arranged a meeting.
   And then I got really busy with life and with work. I
   did two seasons of a Canadian TV show in Budapest. I
   played Hotspur with the RSC for a year, which meant we
   didn't meet up, I forgot all about it until out of the blue,
   nine months ago, Mehmet called me up and said he had
   a free slot in late 2016 early 2017 and did I want it. I said
   yes, of course, the time feels right now, let's do this. But
   I couldn't do one of the plays I'd sent him because, well,
   Mike Bartlett's basically done a much better version of it.
   And in blank verse. That won every award going last year
   in London, and on Broadway. So not that, then. And the
   other one's, well…I've had this idea in my head for a long
   long time, right back to when I lived in Canada, which
   is where I'm from, originally, if you were wondering.
   Which was the story of Vancouver's infamous "Penthouse"
   Nightclub, and the incredible real-life events involving
   Frank Sinatra, an unsolved mafia hit, and the history of
   prostitution and murder in the city, which still resonates to
   this day. To my surprise, Mehmet liked the idea, but then
   we ran into legal problems regarding aspects of the still
   unsolved murder of the Penthouse's boss, Joe Philliponi,
   which was incredibly frustrating, and then sort out of

nowhere, actually because of an article I just happened to be reading online, that's when the idea for *Thebes Land* struck me. I explained it to Mehmet, who gave me the green light, but on the condition that I had something on his desk by the end of the month. Immediately I went to work. When I told Leyla and Laura – the exec team here at the Arcola – that I wanted to have a real-life patricide here on stage, that's so say, someone who had actually killed their father and was serving time, I'm not going to lie, they weren't exactly keen on the idea, but I managed to convince them and we began to initiate all the necessary procedures with the Home Office, or as we very quickly discovered, the Ministry of Justice. To me, the presence of an actual person who had killed their father on stage wasn't a mere detail of the piece but a fundamental component of the concept of the play itself. My interest from the start was to explore patricide in as non-performative a way as possible, to avoid fiction, to create a piece of documentary theatre, that was real in every way. In fact, as you may have already worked out, that's the reason why the set you see behind me consists of a cage. It was one of the conditions set out to us by the Ministry of Justice. In fact, we were only granted authorisation to have a real-life patricide on stage on the condition that we followed very specific security measures, among them, this protective cage, and the locking of any doors to any backstage areas. The letter sent to us by the Ministry demanded "a secured and metallic fence a minimum of three metres in height separating the inmate from the audience". A demand that, as you can see, we have followed to the letter of the law. Now, obviously, at first, I hated the idea of the cage, as did the Arcola. Until the day that I went to Belmarsh prison to have my first encounter with our patricide, with Martin, everyone this is Martin, Martin this is today's audience. And incredibly, our first meeting took place in the prison basketball court. One of those basketball courts that, as tends to be the case in prisons, is surrounded by fencing just like this. As soon as I saw it, I realised we had solved our staging issue. A cage that could both satisfy the Ministry of Justice, and replicate the location of my meetings with Martin. And I'd like to add that Jemima, our set designer, also really liked the fact that, from an artistic point of view, this piece was in large-part inspired and designed by a civil service pen-pusher. In fact, no sooner had I concluded my first meeting with Martin that I remember asking the prison governor if all future meetings with Martin could take place on the basketball court. His answer was yes, that that could happen. Actually. That's perfect. Since we've reached this point of the story, Martin, perhaps we could perform our first encounter. The first time we met. Yes? Okay.

* * *

S: It was an autumn afternoon. Chilly. Windy. The governor took me to the court where Martin was. He was practising. Before entering, I asked the governor whether I could do go in alone. For it to be just the two of us. He said yes. That that was fine. That I could go in alone, but that he was obliged to have a couple of guards watching us at a certain distance. I said I understood perfectly. Martin knew I was coming to see him. He knew someone wanted to talk to him, with a view to writing a play about him. The governor had asked for his consent and he had said yes. At first I chose to talk to Martin through the fence. My idea was that I would wait for him to be the one to invite me onto the court. Hello.

MARTIN: Are you the writer?

S: Yes. That's me.

MARTIN: I thought you'd be older.

S: Aren't you cold?

MARTIN: No. What time is it?

S: It's five o'clock.

MARTIN: Okay. I ain't got much time. You were supposed to be here earlier.

S: Yes. I got held up, I wasn't expecting… The security was… I'm sorry for the delay.

MARTIN: What make is it?

S: Sorry?

MARTIN: I asked what make it is. Your watch.

S: Oh. It's a Casio.

MARTIN: Is it waterproof?

S: I don't know. Maybe.

MARTIN: Or is it water resistant?

S: I… um… It says it's waterproof. To fifty metres.

MARTIN: Has it got a stopwatch?

S: Yes.

MARTIN: And an alarm?

S: Yes. That too. Do you like watches?

MARTIN: What time did you say it was?

S: Five.

MARTIN: Okay.

S: You didn't answer me.

MARTIN: About what?

S: Whether you like watches.

MARTIN: Yes. But I don't like gifts.

S: Neither do I.

MARTIN: I thought you'd be older.

S: Why?

MARTIN: I don't know. They told me a writer would come who wanted to write a book. And that he wanted to speak to me. Wanted to meet me. I thought you'd be old. How old are you?

S: Forty-six.

MARTIN: Forty-six? And me, how old am I?

S: I already know how old you are.

MARTIN: You've read my file?

S: Yes. I have.

MARTIN: And you still wanted to meet me.

S: May I come in?

MARTIN: Aren't you scared?

S: A bit.

MARTIN: If you read my file then you know that I…

S: What?

MARTIN: Nothing.

S: Does it bother you that I read it?

MARTIN: No.

S: It seems as if it does.

MARTIN: Come in if you want.

S: How often do you…?

MARTIN: Every afternoon.

S: Every afternoon?

MARTIN: Well… yeah. Whenever they let me. My cell, yeah. It's really small. And if you don't move around, your body starts to shrink, sort of. The muscles start contracting. And it hurts. It really hurts. You ever been in a cell?

S: No. Never.

MARTIN: The worst is the pain here. In the neck. It starts stiffening up and it kills. No choice but to move.

S: And do you like basketball?

MARTIN: It's the only thing you can do in the fresh air without anyone bothering you. Be alone. Peaceful. You, the ball, the backboard and no one else. No one bothers you.

S: But the guards are always around, right?

MARTIN: They're alright. They just watch. They watch me while I practise.

S: And do you like it?

MARTIN: Like what?

S: That they watch you.

MARTIN: Yes. I don't care. You get used to it here. They're always watching. They never stop watching you. They watch you while you sleep. While you wake up. While you have a piss. While you wash. While you eat. While you practise. See that camera?

S: I hadn't noticed it.

MARTIN: They're always watching. They're watching us now.

S: Right. Of course.

MARTIN: You get used to it eventually.

S: You start to forget about it, right?

MARTIN: No. How can you forget? It's the opposite. You never forget. It's always right there. They're there, on that side and we're here, on this side. And anyway, we all like being watched, don't we? Don't you?

S: I don't know. Depends. It's part of my job. But otherwise…

MARTIN: Do you want to play? Go on. Have a shot.

S: No. Thank you.

MARTIN: No. Thank you.

S: What's so funny?

MARTIN: Nothing. You're alright. It's just that it's been a while since anyone said "No, thank you" to me. I don't know. It's weird.

S: Right.

MARTIN: Do you play?

S: Basketball? No. Never. Only a little, when I was a boy. My father made me play for a year.

MARTIN: Ah…

S: What is it?

MARTIN: No. Nothing. Nothing.

S: Go on. It's okay.

MARTIN: Do you know why I'm here?

S: Yes. I already said. I read your file.

MARTIN: Yes. I know. That's right. Sometimes… I forget. Things. What's your favourite sport, then?

S: I haven't got one.

MARTIN: What? You don't do any sports?

S: I do yoga.

MARTIN: Yoga?

S: And I go swimming twice a week.

MARTIN: In a swimming pool?

S: Yes. In a pool. Where else would I / swim?

MARTIN: And you didn't know your watch was waterproof?

S: No. I didn't. Now that I do, I'll stop taking it off.

MARTIN: What time is it?

S: Don't worry. The governor's given me permission for us to /

MARTIN: It's just there's no more hot water after half five.

S: Oh, right.

MARTIN: And I was expecting you at four.

S: Right. No… It's fine. I would hate to /

MARTIN: It's late.

S: In any case… Today… The idea was… just to meet.

MARTIN: Yes. Yes.

S: Moving forwards, what I'd like is for us to meet twice a week.

MARTIN: Okay.

S: If you agree, that is.

MARTIN: Okay.

S: We can meet here.

MARTIN: Okay.

S: The idea is for us to work together here and then for you to come to the theatre after that.

MARTIN: Okay.

S: To begin with we'll talk. Little by little I'll start writing. Then we'll rehearse. And when we're ready, we'll show our work to an audience.

MARTIN: In the theatre?

S: Yes. Of course. In the theatre. It's all in the project file. You've read my file, right? There will be seven performances a week. The guards will take you to the theatre and bring you back. And there will also be added security in the theatre.

MARTIN: But I'm not…

S: I know. But the Ministry of / Justice…

MARTIN: Nah. I mean. I'm not a what do you call them. I'm not an actor.

S: Oh. Yes. Sorry. Yes. I know. But that doesn't matter.

MARTIN: Something else. I've… never really… been to the theatre.

S: That doesn't matter, either. You have nothing to worry about.

MARTIN: What about the telly bits?

S: The what?

MARTIN: It says we're going to be on the telly too.

S: No no. It's just a stage show. A theatre show.

MARTIN: But it says about the screens. I thought I was going to be on telly.

S: Right. The screens. Yes, there will be screens, but they're nothing to do with being on telly. I'll explain properly later.

MARTIN: Okay.

S: Did they tell you you will be paid? For doing this. For being on stage.

MARTIN: Yes.

S: Good. Do you mind me asking… this project… the idea…
Do you like it?

MARTIN: Yes.

S: Then we can shake hands. It's a deal.

MARTIN: What's your name?

S: Why are you asking if you already know?

MARTIN: Because I felt like asking.

S: You can call me S.

MARTIN: Okay.

S: Are you staying here?

MARTIN: Yes. I have to wait for them to come get me.

S: Well. Okay then. Good luck.

MARTIN: When are you coming back?

S: Next week.

* * *

S: That evening, on the train coming back to town, I began to
write down some notes in my notebook. This notebook
here. I decided to write down as little as possible, some
key impressions, ideas, images. I knew that I didn't want
to start writing writing. I just didn't. I wanted to wait for
the writing to come after our meetings. All I wanted was
to make a note of everything that came into my head
so as not to forget anything. That is why I wrote down
things like BASKETBALL COURT, WATERPROOF
CASIO WATCH, OBSESSION WITH THE TIME, to
which I added OBSESSION WITH TIME in brackets.
Then I wrote CAMERA PERMANENTLY FILMING,
BODY SHRINKING IN THE SMALLNESS OF A
CELL, BODY BEING WATCHED, THREE ARROWS:
WHILST WASHING, WHILST SLEEPING, WHILST
EATING. Beneath that there is a drawing of a backboard

and on the other side a diagram of a desk. Further down it says PATRICIDE, colon, ESTABLISH PARALLELS WITH OEDIPUS, THE BROTHERS KARAMAZOV AND SOME OF FREUD'S WRITINGS. Slightly further down it says WATCH PASOLINI'S OEDIPUS, I never did. Then on the next page there is a question, WHEN DOES ONE TRULY START WRITING A PLAY? And below that question, there is another that asks WHEN DOES ONE TRULY START COMMITTING PATRICIDE? Then a few addresses and telephone numbers, I think they're the contact details for the prison. On this other page there is a brief dialogue that you can tell was written down quickly because of the bad handwriting and it says, hang on a second, DO YOU LIKE IT? LIKE WHAT? BEING WATCHED. YES, I DON'T MIND. And finally there is a page that says HE COULD CALL ME S LIKE THE CHARACTERS IN KAFKA'S NOVELS AND HE COULD BE CALLED MARTIN. Then there is an arrow on which I wrote and underlined MARTIN SANTOS, SANTOS MEANING SAINT, LIKE SAINT MARTIN OF TOURS. The day after that first visit, I received a call from Leyla. She was calling me to let me know that the Ministry of Justice had changed its mind and decided that Martin was not permitted to be in the show after all. Apparently the minister or someone else high up had got wind of the project and had placed an absolute ban on inmates setting foot on a public stage even if our cage was the requisite three metres high. At first I wondered whether I should carry on with the project at all. Mainly, from an artistic point of view, seeing as how Martin's participation, his onstage presence, was crucial to me, but I also saw it as a betrayal of Martin himself. I had told him he'd be participating in a project and this was now denied to him. I asked Leyla if I could have a few days to think about it. After some back and forth, what we decided we would propose to the Ministry was that I would continue to work with Martin on the creation of the piece, and that I would continue to meet him at the prison but that an actor would play him onstage and Martin would be allowed to attend these performances every night as an audience member from the back of the balcony in the company of two police guards. This proposal was put to the Minister, or whoever it was who had decided to fuck us around. (Apologies, it's a technical term.) We received an email the next day, we couldn't believe it, stating the project was authorised to continue, on the condition that Martin would not be on stage and would be handcuffed to a guard throughout the show. Following this reply, with the project back on, the next thing we did was to organise a last minute audition process and it was towards the end of the second day of auditions that I met Freddie, an actor who I then cast in the role of Martin and who is this evening playing both himself and of course Martin. Everyone, this is Freddie. Freddie, the audience. Right. Now that that is all clear, Freddie, perhaps we could perform our first encounter. The first time we met. Yes? Okay.

FREDDIE: Yes. Of course.

* * *

S: The audition took place right here. On this very stage. It was a Wednesday or Thursday afternoon.

FREDDIE: It was a Thursday.

S: Yes. You're right. It was. At the end of a long day. We'd started at 10am, and now it was just before 5pm and Freddie was the last person we were seeing that day. We were meant to have finished at five, so that the evening show, an opera, could get in, but we'd over-run, as you do. I remember that when I saw you walk in, I knew you were my Martin.

FREDDIE: Did you?

S: Yes. Because of this little thing. It had been raining and your hair was wet.

FREDDIE: I'd done it on purpose.

25

S: Done what?

FREDDIE: The wet hair.

S: You purposely let it get rained on?

FREDDIE: No. I wet it before I came in. I went downstairs to the bathroom and wet it. I'd heard you talking to the actor before me about a photo of Martin in which you mentioned wet hair. So I thought it best to wet my hair before coming in.

S: It wasn't because of the rain?

FREDDIE: No. Sorry.

S: You told me you'd gotten your hair all wet in the rain.

FREDDIE: Yes, but I lied. It wasn't true.

S: Nice. So. You came in and instead of sitting down, you just stood.

FREDDIE: Here. Like this.

S: And do you remember what you said to me?

FREDDIE: The first thing I said?

S: Yes. Do you remember?

FREDDIE: That I was afraid I might be late.

S: No. I said. You're all wet. And you said.

FREDDIE: I got caught in the rain.

S: Is it still raining?

FREDDIE: Yes. It's pretty heavy.

S: Do you need a moment?

FREDDIE: I'm alright.

S: Please.

FREDDIE: No. Thank you.

S: No. Thank you.

FREDDIE: What's so funny?

S: Nothing. You're alright. It's just been a while since anyone said no, thank you to me. I don't know. It's weird.

FREDDIE: Right.

S: What's your name?

FREDDIE: It's Frederick. But people call me Freddie.

S: Freddie?

FREDDIE: Yes.

S: Aren't you cold?

FREDDIE: No. No. I'm alright. What time is it?

S: It's five. Exactly five o'clock.

FREDDIE: Don't they want the theatre for the evening show?

S: We're fine for time. Relax.

FREDDIE: Is it waterproof?

S: Sorry?

FREDDIE: No. Nothing. Your Casio, I mean. Is it waterproof or water resistant?

S: Yes. It's waterproof. To fifty metres.

FREDDIE: And / has…

S: Before you ask it has a stopwatch. And an alarm, too. It's funny that you…

FREDDIE: It's just I did the advert. I have the same one. They gave it to me. They said I could keep the one I'd worn. Really nice of them. Normally they /

S: Look /

FREDDIE: Sorry. We can start whenever you're ready.

S: Start what?

FREDDIE: The audition.

S: We've already started.

FREDDIE: Oh. We have?

S: Yes. I think so.

FREDDIE: My name is Freddie. I'm twenty-one years old. I'm six foot one. The casting said you had to be over six foot one but I'm exactly six foot one. Is that /

27

S: It's fine. Tell me. Do you know how to play basketball?

FREDDIE: Yes. Well. My agent /

S: Do you or don't you?

FREDDIE: I…

S: It says here / that you…

FREDDIE: I played at school. I was in the school team.

S: Here. Show me.

FREDDIE: What?

S: Do you know how to dribble?

(FREDDIE dribbles.)

S: Okay. You're not that bad.

FREDDIE: Thank you. But this is easy. Anyone can do it.

S: And a bit faster?

FREDDIE: Like this?

S: Yes.

(FREDDIE dribbles faster.)

S: And faster?

FREDDIE: Faster?

S: Go on.

FREDDIE: I'll try. *(FREDDIE dribbles faster.)* Like this?

S: Yes that's good.

FREDDIE: Thank you.

S: Don't stop.

(FREDDIE dribbles.)

S: You're better than I was expecting. Okay. Now, let's try a few shots.

FREDDIE: Yes. Of course…. From here?

S: Wherever you like.

(FREDDIE reacts to getting it or not getting it.)

S: And again.

FREDDIE: Alright.

S: Good.

FREDDIE: That was an easy one. I'll try a bit further back.

S: Go on.

FREDDIE: Missed that one.

S: It wasn't too far off.

FREDDIE: Can I try again?

S: Yes. Of course.

FREDDIE: Thank you. I mean. Alright.

S: Not bad. You're doing well.

FREDDIE: I'll practise. I'm a fast learner. I like training. It's my favourite thing about acting. Learning new skills. *(Takes another shot.)*

S: Alright. Enough. Have a seat.

FREDDIE: No. No. I'm alright thanks.

S: Have a seat. Please. You'll be more comfortable.

FREDDIE: Alright.

S: And you're at which school?

FREDDIE: RADA.

S: RADA?

FREDDIE: Yeah.

S: Okay. And when did you finish?

FREDDIE: I'm actually still in the third year. But we're allowed to audition for professional projects. I asked my head of year. They said it was okay.

S: Okay. Fine. So, tell me, why did you come to the audition?

FREDDIE: Well. I really liked that TV series you did.

S: Which one? Actually, it doesn't matter.

FREDDIE: And I've seen you on stage and I really like the way you act.

S: Okay. But aside from that, from seeing me on TV or the way I act, tell me a bit about what it is that sparked your interest in this particular project.

FREDDIE: Well... A bit of everything?

S: But what in particular?

FREDDIE: Well. The idea.

S: What idea?

FREDDIE: I don't know. The idea of playing this guy.

S: Why?

FREDDIE: I don't know. It's something that... It intrigues me.

S: What?

FREDDIE: Patricide.

S: And why does it intrigue you?

FREDDIE: I don't know... The act of killing one's own father. It's something I find sort of impossible to comprehend, right? I don't know. I don't think I'd ever be able to. I could never do it. Could you?

S: No. I don't think so. I don't think I could.

FREDDIE: And then, at the same time, you also never know. Sat here, peaceful, it's easy to say one could never kill one's own father, but then...

S: Then, what?

FREDDIE: I don't know. You never know what could happen. You never know what you're capable of in certain situations. How you might react in certain circumstances.

S: I'd like you to read something I'm going to give you.

FREDDIE: Is it part of the play?

S: No. Well. I don't know. Maybe. I haven't decided yet.

FREDDIE: Okay. Do you want me to perform it? If I can have a minute / just to look over it.

S: No. No. No. Just give it a go.

FREDDIE: Okay.

S: Go ahead.

FREDDIE: What, now?

S: Whenever you're ready.

FREDDIE: "Sphinx. In Greek mythology, the Sphinx was
represented as having a lion's body with two breasts,
a woman's face and the wings of a bird of prey. They
say it came from Ethiopia to bring terror to the city of
Thebes, sent by the goddess Hera to punish the city for
the homosexual love of King Laius for young Chrysippus.
Some scholars suggest this may have been the first
homosexual relationship in history. The Sphinx lived in
one of the mountains of the city of Thebes, destroying
those who were unable to solve its riddle. The riddle was
as follows: "What is the animal that walks first on four legs,
then two and finally three?" Many failed to solve it, until
Oedipus, the forgotten son of the now dead King Laius /
and…

S: Dead because Oedipus himself had killed him, of course,
not knowing that Laius was actually his father. Sorry. I
interrupted you. Go on.

FREDDIE: Many failed to solve it, until Oedipus, the forgotten
son of the now dead King Laius and the widowed Queen
Jocasta came to Thebes and answered, saying "In your
riddle you speak of man who drags himself on all fours
as an infant, then walks on two and sees himself obliged
as an old man to lean on a stick, which is then like a third
leg". Upon hearing Oedipus's answer, the Sphinx is said
to have leaped to its death from the highest part of the
mountain. As his reward, Oedipus married Queen Jocasta,
not knowing she was his real mother and became the new
king of Thebes". And that was it.

S: Thank you.

FREDDIE: That was it, right? Because then I left. And then five
minutes later, or at least it felt like five minutes later, you
called me to say I'd got the part.

S: Yes.

FREDDIE: You never told me why, exactly.

S: I don't think I knew at the time.

FREDDIE: What about now?

S: Now?

FREDDIE: Was it because of the wet hair?

S: Yes. But there was something else. Actually, when you finished reading... Just now you didn't play the end of the scene quite right. It wasn't exactly like that.

FREDDIE: It wasn't?

S: No. After you finished reading, you said something.

FREDDIE: I don't remember.

S: You said something about Laius and Oedipus.

FREDDIE: Did I?

S: Yes. You told me that you'd just realised that Oedipus didn't really know he was killing his father when he did it.

FREDDIE: Oh yes. I remember.

S: It was just before you left.

FREDDIE: That's right. I... I only just realised.

S: Sorry?

FREDDIE: I just realised something.

S: What?

FREDDIE: That Oedipus didn't actually know it was his father. I mean, when he kills Laius, he thinks he's killing someone else. He doesn't know he's killing his own father. In actuality... I don't know if he's a true patricide. Yes. No. Hang on. That's not what I meant. What I meant is that really, he's a patricide who doesn't know he's a patricide.

S: Yes. In a manner of speaking...

FREDDIE: He's like a false patricide. Like, it wasn't his vocation. He didn't premeditate it. He isn't a one hundred percent bonafide patricide.

S: Bonafide patricide.

FREDDIE: Yeah, not the real deal.

S: But the man he kills is his father, however you look at it, even if he, Oedipus, doesn't know it.

FREDDIE: Yes. But when he does it, he isn't aware of it. He doesn't actually know what he's doing. In any case, it's arguable, right?

S: Then I said yes. That it could in effect be argued. That's when Freddie headed to the door, said goodbye and left.

FREDDIE: Then that's why... It was because of what I said.

S: That was a big factor, yes.

FREDDIE: Should I close the door behind me?

S: Yes. Thank you.

* * *

S: Two days after casting Freddie, I went back to the prison. I wanted to tell Martin myself about the problem we'd come up against. The guards led me to the basketball court and told me to wait. He'd gone to the infirmary. I then waited a few minutes until he arrived. His left hand was bandaged.

* * *

MARTIN: It's nothing.

S: What happened?

MARTIN: I sprained it a bit.

S: Playing?

MARTIN: Yes. But it's nothing.

S: Does it hurt?

MARTIN: A bit. Have you been waiting long?

S: No. No. I only just arrived.

MARTIN: They already told me...

33

S: What?

MARTIN: That they won't let me.

S: Who told you?

MARTIN: The governor.

S: I wanted to tell you myself.

MARTIN: But they already told me. They don't want me to be on stage.

S: It's a security issue.

MARTIN: Yes. Yes. They explained everything. It's fine.

S: They've agreed you can come to the performances. As an audience member. And you would still be paid a fee. Not the whole...

MARTIN: Yes. They said. But it's not the same.

S: Well... You won't be able to go on stage, but at least you'll be able to come to the theatre. You'll be with us every night. In the balcony. And on stage, in your place, there will be an actor.

MARTIN: Like in the cinema?

S: Yes.

MARTIN: Who?

S: An actor I've chosen.

MARTIN: And does he look like me?

S: A bit.

MARTIN: Because he has to look like me, right?

S: No. Not necessarily.

MARTIN: But, does he look like me or not?

S: Yes. He looks like you. He looks a lot like you.

MARTIN: What's his name?

S: Freddie.

MARTIN: And he's...? He's going to act like me?

S: He's going to tell the story in your place.

MARTIN: What story?

S: Yours.

MARTIN: He's going to copy me?

S: Well... No. That isn't how it works. You'll understand when you come and see us in the theatre.

MARTIN: But if he's going to play me, then he has to copy me. So he'll be like me. I mean. Right?

S: He's going to be you. No scratch that. He's going to draw inspiration from you.

MARTIN: Draw what?

S: Draw inspiration... Do you understand?

MARTIN: No.

S: Okay... I'm going to try to explain it to you. He isn't going to copy you, imitate you. He's an actor. And an actor's job is not to copy. He is going to create what is known as a character. He's going to draw inspiration, that is to say, he's going to start with you, from your story, from everything you are going to tell me, to create a character himself.

MARTIN: But then it won't be me.

S: Well... No. It will be a character. A character created with you as a basis. No one but you can be you, really.

MARTIN: Is that why you wanted me to act in the theatre?

S: Of course. If you had been able to do it, then you would have been both yourself and your character at the same time.

MARTIN: This is fucked.

S: Well. But it's alright. You'll still be there.

MARTIN: So I'll just be sat there?

S: You are sitting there.

MARTIN: What?

S: Up there, on the balcony.

MARTIN: Okay. But I won't be on stage.

S: Well, you'll be there in some fashion. Your story will be on stage. You are what we're going to be talking about.

MARTIN: And will he come?

S: Who?

MARTIN: What did you say his name was?

S: Who?

MARTIN: The actor.

S: Freddie?

MARTIN: Yes. Will he come to see me?

S: No. I don't think so. You know… It isn't easy coming here. Getting in. You need lots of permissions. Lots of authorisations.

MARTIN: But if he don't know me, I don't understand how he's going to do it. How is he going to play me, if he's never met me?

S: Well… He'll have the script.

MARTIN: What script?

S: The one I'm going to write. The one I'm writing. And he's going to work from that script.

MARTIN: And what's going to be in the script?

S: I don't know. Lots of things. Your story. Everything we're going to talk about. The things you're going to tell me. Our meetings. Everything we're talking about now, for example, could also be in the script.

MARTIN: What?

S: Everything we're talking about now.

MARTIN: What? This?

S: Yes.

MARTIN: So everything I say is going to be in the script.

S: No. Not everything. Some things.

MARTIN: What we talk about? My questions?

S: Yes.

MARTIN: Just like that? Word for word?

S: Well. No. I change it afterwards. Change some things. Modify it a bit. I'm never going to make an exact transcription of our conversation.

MARTIN: A what?

S: A transcription. A duplicate. A copy. The interesting part about writing this is actually making the slight changes. Changing little things to /

MARTIN: You mean you're going to make some things up.

S: Yes. Of course.

MARTIN: So, nothing is nothing.

S: What do you mean nothing is nothing?

MARTIN: Yeah. It won't even be me. He don't even know me. And what we talked about won't even be what we talked about. You're going to change everything.

S: Yes. No. In a manner of speaking. Everything will be moved around a bit.

MARTIN: And if, you know, if there's something I want left out?

S: You tell me.

MARTIN: I tell you and you take it out.

S: We talk about it.

MARTIN: But, if I don't want it in there?

S: Relax, there won't be anything in there you don't like.

MARTIN: I am relaxed.

S: Okay. Good.

MARTIN: It's just that in case there is something that…

S: Don't worry.

MARTIN: You know… Some things… I don't know if I would like…

S: Which things, for example?

MARTIN: I don't know. You know why I'm in here. You told me you knew. That you'd read my file.

S: Yes.

MARTIN: Well… There are things that… I don't know. It's not easy. I don't know if I want everyone looking at them afterwards.

S: What things?

MARTIN: And… Now that I know you're going to write everything we talk about, I feel weird about telling you.

S: I already told you I'm not going to write anything you don't want me to. It'll be as if we were writing the script together.

MARTIN: Yeah. Yeah. But all the same. Some things aren't easy to tell.

S: Yes. I can imagine. But you can be sure I won't write anything you don't want me to. And besides, you also don't have to tell me anything you don't want to.

MARTIN: I… killed my dad.

S: Yes. I know.

MARTIN: So… There are things… There are things that are hard to say.

S: So don't say them. Just talk to me about what you want to talk about.

MARTIN: When are you coming back?

S: Soon. The day after tomorrow.

MARTIN: Yesterday when they told me I wouldn't be able to play myself in the theatre, I was scared.

S: Of what?

MARTIN: That you wouldn't come back.

S: I'm going to be coming twice a week. If they / let me.

MARTIN: They won't. We only have permission for one visit every / two weeks.

S: It's been authorised.

MARTIN: Is it?

S: So long as you're willing…

MARTIN: I'm here. Easy.

S: Ah… Yesterday I was looking at the origins of your name.

MARTIN: What?

S: What your name means. What Martin means. And, do you know what it means?

MARTIN: No.

S: War. Warrior. It's Latin. It comes from Martinus which means belonging to the god Mars. Do you know who the god Mars was?

MARTIN: No idea.

S: He was the god of War.

MARTIN: Sick.

S: What's that?

MARTIN: This?

S: Yes.

MARTIN: It's a rosary. I always have it on me. We're not really allowed it. It says so in the rules. No watches. No rings. No chains. No bracelets. They say we could use them to attack each other. But they let us wear rosaries. Religious.

S: See? For example, here I'm going to have you say something like… It's a rosary. I always have it on me. But to that I'm going to add… It's made of jasmine petals.

MARTIN: What is?

S: The rosary.

MARTIN: Jasmine petals? Never heard of them.

S: Didn't you know? Lots of them are made of jasmine petals.

MARTIN: This one isn't…

S: But now it is.

MARTIN: My mum gave it to me. That's why I always have it on me.

S: You never take it off?

MARTIN: No. Never. That's why I always smell of jasmine.

* * *

SECOND QUARTER

S: As soon as I got in that night, I started looking for anything I could find about Martin online. After Googling his name, I found hundreds of thousands of links. Everything from news stories to press clippings to an endless stream of social media accounts that frequently mentioned him. Every now and then a picture came up. Almost always the same one. It was a photo of him as a boy where, incredibly, he was pictured with his father. This is the photo. They're at the beach. They'd taken it while on holiday, Martin explained to me some time later. And as you can see, Martin is on his father's shoulders with his hands on his head. They are both smiling. Father and son. Every time that image came up on my computer, I couldn't stop thinking about two things. Firstly, how the press could be so cynical. In writing about Martin as a patricide, they had stubbornly elected to use a photo that, as you can see, is overflowing with affection between father and son. I think I would rather have seen the classic images of the condemned man arriving at or leaving court on the day of his sentencing. Or a mugshot. But not this photo in which they both appear momentarily complicit. The second thing I couldn't stop thinking about was who had taken the photo. Of course in my head it was his mother. I talked about that photo with Martin several times in our meetings. But I never asked him who had taken it. I never found the courage to ask him. And I don't think he felt like telling me, either. The only thing he would talk to me about was his still intact memory of the warmth of his father's head against his chest and the sharp smell of salt in his father's hair.

* * *

FREDDIE: So they were on holiday?

S: Yes.

FREDDIE: How old is he?

S: Who?

FREDDIE: Martin.

S: He's ten.

FREDDIE: And his father?

S: Twenty years older than him.

FREDDIE: Thirty years old?

S: Yes. He had him when he was twenty.

FREDDIE: And does he remember?

S: Remember what?

FREDDIE: This photo.

S: Yes, of course.

FREDDIE: Which beach is it?

S: That he can't remember.

FREDDIE: Wow. Does he have siblings?

S: No. He's an only child. How's the basketball going?

FREDDIE: Good, yeah.

S: Are you going every day?

FREDDIE: Every morning.

S: Perfect.

FREDDIE: Is the idea that I'm going to play onstage?

S: I don't know. Maybe.

FREDDIE: Do you like it?

S: Like what?

FREDDIE: Basketball.

S: No. I don't know. I neither like it, nor dislike it. I'm utterly indifferent to it. In fact, I hardly know anything about it. I'm literally just starting to learn about it. The other day I asked Martin to write me a list of basketball terms. To get to know the vocabulary a bit. He said he'd make it for me.

FREDDIE: I read in an interview you gave the other day that your father played basketball professionally.

S: Yes.

FREDDIE: I bet that's the reason you decided to stage the piece around basketball, right?

S: No no, that has nothing to do with it. I spoke about my father in the interview because… The decision to use a basketball court as the performance space is because it's the place where I always meet Martin at the prison.

FREDDIE: Does he play a lot?

S: Whenever they let him.

FREDDIE: And is he good?

S: Let's just say you have some catching up to do.

FREDDIE: I can't wait to go.

S: Go where?

FREDDIE: To the prison. To meet him.

S: Oh no. I don't think it's a good idea for the two of you to meet for the moment. I don't think it would do either of you any good.

FREDDIE: Oh.

S: I'm afraid your visit could confuse him even further. There are things he has trouble understanding. The other day he was having trouble comprehending the concept of representation. He didn't understand what acting is. He got everything mixed up in his head. The idea of imitation, simulation, copying.

FREDDIE: I sometimes get it all mixed up myself.

S: Yes, but he was different. He was unable to properly grasp the difference between presenting and representing. He asked me how it could be possible for someone to portray him without having met him personally. Or how someone would play him if they didn't look like him. As if he weren't aware of the distance that always exists between the model and the copy when something is being represented.

FREDDIE: And… It isn't something that's that easy to grasp.

S: Really?

FREDDIE: Yeah

S: It's so obvious to me. It's the basis for all our work. Everything depends on it.

FREDDIE: On what?

S: That distance.

FREDDIE: Maybe.

S: Actually, to me that distance is the reason that art is always better than reality.

FREDDIE: What? Always?

S: I'm certain of it.

FREDDIE: Really?

S: Yes. I think so. Absolutely.

FREDDIE: I don't.

S: Tell me something, have you read his official file?

FREDDIE: Yes. I started on it.

S: You don't have to read all of it. I highlighted the important parts.

FREDDIE: I'm still at the beginning.

S: It gets more interesting.

FREDDIE: Are you going to use them?

S: Yes. Almost certainly. I'll probably use the forensic reports.

FREDDIE: The script, then… Are you still… Have you started writing it?

S: Yes.

FREDDIE: After every meeting with him, you get a bit further along.

S: And after every rehearsal with you, as well.

FREDDIE: Ah, okay. Can I see it?

S: Not yet. It's not ready. I'm still gathering material.
Everything I can find. I'll see how I organise it later.

FREDDIE: Everything?

S: Yes. No. Not everything. I'm trying to gather everything
that could be related, in one way or another. What we just
talked about, for example, about how a representation of
the world can be better than the world itself, right, that, I
can use. Or the photo we were just looking at. Or some
of the reports from the file. Or the piece about the Sphinx
you read at your audition.

FREDDIE: Who wrote that?

S: I don't know actually. I got it from Wikipedia that morning.

FREDDIE: And when are you going to put it all together?

S: Right now, I'm just trying to give it a shape.

FREDDIE: So you're pulling the best bits of your interviews
with him.

S: Yes. Of course. And some things, I'll make up. But it's also
the things I see. The things I hear. The other day, for
example, on the minibus that takes me from the prison to
the train station, the whole way the driver was playing that
Whitney Houston song, *I Have Nothing.* Do you know it?

FREDDIE: No.

S: You've never seen *The Bodyguard*?

FREDDIE: No.

S: You're too young, I guess.

FREDDIE: Is it famous?

S: Seriously. Kevin Costner. Whitney. I will always love you.
On the runway.

FREDDIE: No.

S: Okay. Doesn't matter. The point is. I listened to *I Have
Nothing* in the prison minibus. And since I couldn't get it

out of my head the rest of the night, I thought maybe we
could use it in the show.

FREDDIE: Are you going to use stuff from this too. *(Picks up a
copy of Vancouver's Legendary Penthouse Nightclub.)*

S: No. No. That's for a different project. That's got nothing
to do with this. It's a piece I'm working on for another
theatre. Look, we're going off track. Perhaps we could start
working from the holiday photo.

FREDDIE: Yes. The photo…

S: What's the matter?

FREDDIE: No. Nothing. I'm thinking it's completely
understandable for him to be worried about the thought of
someone else portraying him.

S: Yes. Perhaps.

FREDDIE: I think I'd feel a bit like him if… I don't know if I'd
like someone else playing me.

S: There's a reason you're an actor, right?

FREDDIE: I guess.

S: Shall we get started?

FREDDIE: Sure.

* * *

S: Well. What do you feel like telling me?

MARTIN: Do I have to talk to you about…? About what
happened…?

S: No. No. Not necessarily. You can talk to me about anything
you like. And if you want to talk to me about what
happened, you can do that too.

MARTIN: And you're going to ask me questions?

S: Yes. Sometimes. But today I'd rather you talk to me about
whatever you want to talk about.

MARTIN: I don't know. I don't know what I feel like talking about.

S: Would you rather I ask you a different question?

MARTIN: Yeah.

S: Okay. Let me think.

MARTIN: But don't ask me difficult questions. Remember, I didn't even finish secondary school.

S: Okay. There you go. You could tell me about that, for example.

MARTIN: About what?

S: About school. How far did you get?

MARTIN: Not very far. I didn't do my GSCEs.

S: But did you like school?

MARTIN: Sometimes. I liked some of the teachers. But I wasn't a good student.

S: Why?

MARTIN: I... I didn't understand. Things. What they were talking about.

S: And why did you drop out?

MARTIN: For that reason. I don't know. One day I just stopped going. I stopped going and that was it. I regret it now. Maybe if I'd finished... I don't know. Everything would have been different. I wouldn't have got sick in the head. Because that's what they say. That I'm ill. Up here, see? That's how it is.

S: Is that what they tell you?

MARTIN: I have a psychologist. He sees me once a month. But I don't tell him anything. He says I'm mentally ill. That that's why... That's why what happened happened.

S: But that's got nothing to do with how far you got in school.

MARTIN: But I'm ill.

S: You don't become ill because you stop going to school early.

MARTIN: Yeah, but I'm not well. In my head. It's a psychological issue. A chemical imbalance. That's why I take pills.

S: Yes. Yes. I understand that you're ill. What I was trying to say is that not having finished school doesn't make you ill.

MARTIN: Yeah but it does. Because you start going stupid. My dad always said that.

S: Said what?

MARTIN: That I was stupid. That leaving school was making me even more stupid than I already was.

S: Sometimes parents say that to their children. He probably wasn't happy about you leaving school.

MARTIN: Maybe. But my dad said it all the time. You're stupid. You're a retard. You're no good. He was always saying the same thing. You're even more of an idiot since you left school. You're useless. You're a waste of space. Then I started to get ill. Now do you understand?

S: Do you know you can go to school here?

MARTIN: Yes. But I don't... I can't get anything through my thick skull.

S: Why don't you try?

MARTIN: I did. I tried but I didn't understand nothing. The teachers talked but I didn't understand the words they were saying. They used difficult words. Like you.

S: Do you sometimes not understand what I'm saying?

MARTIN: I... Sometimes you use sort of complicated words.

S: Like what?

MARTIN: I... I don't know.

S: But you have to let me know. Whenever I say something you don't understand, you have to tell me right away.

MARTIN: There's lots of people I don't understand.

S: But that's why... A teacher is there to explain. To explain the words you don't understand.

MARTIN: Yes. I know. But it's embarrassing.

S: What is?

MARTIN: I… Asking questions all the time. You feel… I don't know. Haven't you ever been embarrassed?

S: Yes. Well. No. Well, yes. Sometimes, yes. But for different reasons.

MARTIN: We're all embarrassed about different things. Some people don't like being naked in the shower, for example. But that doesn't embarrass me. What about you?

S: What?

MARTIN: Are you embarrassed of being naked in the showers at the pool?

S: No. Why would I be embarrassed?

MARTIN: I… Usually if guys are embarrassed about being naked in the showers, it's because they've got a little dick.

S: The point is you shouldn't be embarrassed to ask something you don't know.

MARTIN: Easy for you to say.

S: Yes. I know.

MARTIN: You're a teacher, right?

S: Yes. Amongst other things, yes, I have taught. I teach.

MARTIN: In a school.

S: Yes. At drama schools.

MARTIN: So you've got pupils.

S: Yes. Students. Well, acting students in my case.

MARTIN: You must be clever then.

S: That doesn't mean anything.

MARTIN: I mean you must have worked really hard. Studied. Read loads.

S: Yes. I have read quite a lot. But all you really need is perseverance.

MARTIN: See? That's a word I don't understand, for example.

S: Perseverance? You don't know what it means?

MARTIN: No.

S: Okay. So. It means you need to be constant, patient… it's like endurance. You understand endurance, right?

MARTIN: Yeah.

S: Well, that's what perseverance means.

MARTIN: So why didn't you say what you really need is endurance, then?

S: Yes, I could have used that word, but I preferred to use the other one. When one knows several words, one can choose.

MARTIN: But when you only know a few, you can't. That's the problem. And that's why it's hard to understand you. That's why we never understand when you talk to us. Because I'm not the only one this happens to. The same thing happens to nearly everyone in here.

S: Well, but all you have to do is ask, right? Now, for example, you know new word. Next time, instead of saying patience or endurance, you'll be able to say perseverance.

MARTIN: You're talking to me like a teacher.

S: Yes. You're right. And I don't like it.

MARTIN: I like it.

S: Why?

MARTIN: I don't know. Listening to you talk like that. You explaining things to me.

S: But I'm not a teacher.

MARTIN: But you told me that you were.

S: What I meant is that I'm not your teacher.

MARTIN: You could be…

S: No. Look. I'm not here as a teacher. I'm here to talk to you. To get to know you. To write a play as I already explained. But not to be your teacher.

MARTIN: You want me to stay stupid.

49

S: Why do you say that?

MARTIN: Because you're telling me you don't want to be my teacher.

S: You're mixing everything up. You have a slight tendency to muddle things.

MARTIN: I didn't understand that last sentence.

S: Okay. You mix everything up in your head.

MARTIN: And?

S: You know perfectly well I'm not here to be your teacher.

MARTIN: Yes. I know.

S: Why would you say I want you to stay stupid?

MARTIN: I was joking.

S: It isn't a very nice thing to say.

MARTIN: I said it without thinking.

S: What I can do is talk to the governor to see if he'll let you enrol on a course.

MARTIN: See?

S: What?

MARTIN: Problem solved. You help sign me up for a course and that's that. You can rest easy.

S: I don't understand.

MARTIN: Course you don't.

S: What's wrong?

MARTIN: Nothing.

S: Something's wrong.

MARTIN: It's just… I don't know. Sometimes I think that, deep down, you lot hate us.

S: Why do you say you lot?

MARTIN: Because you're all the same.

S: Who?

MARTIN: You lot.

S: What are you talking about?

MARTIN: How you lot hate us.

S: You're delusional.

MARTIN: I don't know what that word means.

S: I don't hate you.

MARTIN: Yes, you do.

S: If I did I wouldn't be here.

MARTIN: I don't know about that.

S: I do.

MARTIN: You're only here for your ego.

S: Why would you say that?

MARTIN: Because it's true. You're only here to write your
    book. So I'll tell you things.

S: If that were all I was after, I could have just read your file.

MARTIN: No. That's not true. What you want is for me to
    tell you what isn't in the file. What I didn't tell the others.
    What I never told anyone. That things that…

S: Alright. Maybe. Maybe that's true.

MARTIN: That's what you want.

S: And?

MARTIN: And I don't actually matter to you.

S: What do you know?

MARTIN: I could be anyone. All you really care about is what
    happened. What I did. How I did it. What I did it with.
    How many blows. Where I hit my dad. What his last
    words were. For me to properly tell you how I did it. And
    tell you why I did it. What my reasons were. And that…
    That's the only part of me that interests you.

S: Excuse me?

MARTIN: And what you care most about is writing it well.
    Writing a good book or play or whatever you call it. For
    people to say: How impressive! What a great play! That's

all you care about. And to be able to tell people that you wrote it by coming to meet with the killer. And that you wrote it on a basketball court. That's all you care about.

S: I don't understand where all of this is coming from. We can stop this now if you want. Actually I think it's for the best.

MARTIN: What? Are you scared?

S: No. Not at all. That isn't it. I think things have become muddled. I don't think you understood properly.

MARTIN: And?

S: I think I'm going to go.

MARTIN: No. Wait. Don't go.

S: I think we're done for today.

MARTIN: But don't go.

S: I don't understand what just happened. I don't understand why you said the things you said.

MARTIN: I'm sorry.

S: No. It's not a question of being sorry. I don't know. It's as though you got everything mixed up in your head.

MARTIN: I told you I'm not clever. Things get muddled. I find it hard to understand. Everything gets confused. Really. I'm sorry.

S: It's fine.

MARTIN: Everything I said, I just said it, without thinking.

S: Some of the things you said are true, but others aren't.

MARTIN: Don't be angry. I don't want you to leave and be angry.

S: No. I'm not angry.

MARTIN: Are you coming back?

S: I don't know.

MARTIN: I promise I'm going to make you that list.

S: What list?

MARTIN: The one you asked me to make with basketball words.

S: Okay.

MARTIN: But… Are you coming back?

S: You said some things…

MARTIN: Yes. I know. I get it. What I want to know is…

S: Yes. I also get it. You want to know whether I'm coming back or not.

MARTIN: To know if I should wait for you. Get it?

S: On Thursday. I'll come on Thursday.

MARTIN: I'll be here. I'll be waiting.

* * *

S: I didn't go again that week. I needed a few more days before seeing him again. When I called to let the governor know I wouldn't be going that Thursday, I took the opportunity to tell him that I thought it would be a good idea for Martin to return to his studies. He said yes. That he thought it was a good idea. But that Martin was generally disinterested in group activities. He was a recluse, he preferred solitude. When he said that about Martin, I felt like changing my mind and telling him I would go see him after all. But it wouldn't have been, well, I wouldn't have come across well, if I was to tell him one thing then change my mind three minutes later. It did occur to me, however, to ask him to tell Martin that I wouldn't be there because I was ill and that I'd be back as soon as I was better. Before hanging up he asked me if Martin had spoken to me of his visions yet. I told him no. That we'd never spoken about it. And that I didn't actually have any idea what he was talking about. He told me that Martin had visions.

* * *

FREDDIE: Visions?

S: Yes. That's what he told me. But I'd prefer we spoke about that in another scene.

FREDDIE: Okay. It's just that you just brought it up.

S: Yes. Yes. It's true. It's just on my mind a lot. When you start writing you want to touch on every subject. But it's best if we leave the visions for later. It doesn't feel like the right moment now.

FREDDIE: No problem.

S: I'd prefer to work on the forensic reports for a bit.

FREDDIE: I took them home.

S: Did you read them?

FREDDIE: Yes. They're pretty intense. Especially the photos.

S: Yes. They're not very nice.

FREDDIE: And the thing about stabbing him twenty-one times stayed with me.

S: It's pretty shocking, right?

FREDDIE: Has he told you about it yet?

S: About what?

FREDDIE: I don't know. About what it was like. How it went down.

S: No. And I doubt he will. That isn't what I'm after, actually. I don't know if I could stand to hear it.

FREDDIE: And the place where he did it... The kitchen. It's weird, isn't it?

S: It only took place there because that's where they happened to be when they fought that morning.

FREDDIE: And it all kicked off because of what the father said? Because of the insult?

S: Apparently he called him a whore. Well... That might have been what set him off. But I don't think it's the only reason he stabbed his father twenty-one times.

FREDDIE: He just said that, all of a sudden, out of the blue?

S: According to other information, the father had already called him a whore on other occasions. Even in public.

FREDDIE: Wow.

S: Martin had started prostituting himself. He had left school. Then he worked different jobs for a few months at a time but always got fired. And in the end, just a few months after his mother's death, he'd started prostituting himself. At first he operated in hotels or in the clients' cars, but then he started bringing them home.

FREDDIE: Which is how the father found out…

S: That isn't clear. Some say the father had known for a while. That someone had told him. Anyway the point is he took to calling Martin a whore whenever they argued.

FREDDIE: And why were they arguing that morning?

S: That's explained in one of the final hearings in the report. Here it is. It was on a Sunday. When Martin got home in the early hours, his father was in the kitchen. He'd got up for a glass of water and upon seeing him come home, looked at him and supposedly said: you couldn't even remember to buy milk. Martin said something back and the father apparently launched straight in and called him a whore. And well, that's when Martin is meant to have grabbed a fork and stabbed him twenty one times. Martin even said in the report that, even as he was stabbing him with the fork, his father kept saying Can't you see? Can't you see you're a whore that can't even remember to buy milk?

FREDDIE: …?

S: Yes. I know. It really lends itself to psychoanalysis. The bit with the milk, I mean. Mother's milk. Seminal milk. Milk that nourishes. Milk that gives life. Barthes would have had a field day.

FREDDIE: Who?

S: Barthes. Roland Barthes. The French semiologist… You haven't heard of him.

FREDDIE: No. Should I have?

S: Yes. You should have. He's written some fascinating essays about theatre.

FREDDIE: Okay.

S: You know, I'm not surprised you haven't read him. His ideas are difficult. Sometimes I ask the students I work with what they're reading and... Now there's this tendency to read easy things. God forbid they should come into contact with a complex idea. Was it like that for you?

FREDDIE: What are you trying to say?

S: That you should read more Barthes. You know what. I'll bring you some of his books tomorrow.

FREDDIE: Great.

S: Good. Now. Do you think we could look at some of the crime scene photos? I'd like to show them on the screens.

FREDDIE: You... You want to show them to the audience?

S: Maybe.

FREDDIE: That might be interesting, but... do you think they'll allow it?

S: We'll have to ask for permission.

FREDDIE: And if you don't get it?

S: We can fake them. Show the audience some different photos. Haven't you seen all the crime scene photos online?

FREDDIE: No.

S: There are hundreds. Thousands even.

FREDDIE: But, are they real? Of real crimes?

S: Of course. At least I think so. There's a whole black market for images of crime scene photos. Worse case, we'll take some photos from the web, put them up on the screens, cover their faces with black squares and hey presto.

FREDDIE: That's not a bad idea.

S: And we'll make something up to explain why we had to cover the faces. As a mark of respect or maybe something else that sounds more legalistic. That way we can pass off any crime scene photos we find as photos of Martin's crime.

FREDDIE: Some of the photos are really powerful.

S: There are three in particular I find very interesting.

FREDDIE: Is this one of them?

S: Yes. That's one of them. Shocking, isn't it? Anna, could you? Thanks. No stop. Go back. Actually. Wait a moment. Before showing any of the images we're about to project, I am obliged to make an important clarification. In fact, I am just going to read this letter from our friends at the Ministry of Justice *'By law, it is strictly forbidden to represent and/or show an actual corpse on stage, be it by its physical presence, or by its audiovisual projection, with some provisions being taken for the latter. In other words, an actual corpse may not appear onstage and its audiovisual representation may only be authorised if two thirds of the face are obscured by a black square and that the audience is made aware of the nature of said images in advance of any projection.'* Well, seeing as I'm obliged to give you prior warning, we are about to project three images of Martin's father. If anyone wishes to leave, you may do so now and we'll come and get you back in about a minute's time. Alternatively, you can also close your eyes. Does anyone wish to leave? Very well. Anna. This is the first photo. As has just been explained, we were obliged to obscure the victim's face with a black square covering two-thirds of the face. What interests me about this photo is that you can quite clearly see the sheer amount of wounds across the entire body and that, in some way, all these wounds remind me of Andrea Mantegna's *St Sebastians*, where the body of the saint appears excessively damaged in order to highlight his pain and suffering. Moving on to the second photo, Anna, what grabs me in this photo are the father's open eyes. I don't think he closed them at any point. That he witnessed his death in its entirety. I don't know. The two open eyes make me think that he was

57

present as an audience member throughout. And finally, thank you Anna, this third photo intrigues me because of where the body is. I was struck by the image of his body leaning against the refrigerator door. Especially because, after killing him, Martin confessed to have opened the refrigerator more than once to retrieve various things. I'm shocked by the image of the son opening the fridge with his own father's body, his corpse, pressed up against it. Thank you. If you'd closed your eyes, you can now open them.

FREDDIE: He didn't call the police until midday?

S: Yes. He spent all morning at home with his father's body up against the fridge. He showered. Ate breakfast. Watched television. Went back to the kitchen because he was hungry. Made himself a peach smoothie. Drank it. And only then did he go to the telephone, call the police and tell the first person he spoke to: I just killed my father by stabbing him twenty-one times with a fork.

FREDDIE: You mean he counted them.

S: It would appear so.

FREDDIE: I'm still thinking about the photos.

S: Disturbing, eh?

FREDDIE: Yes.

S: But they're also great. Technically, I mean. Whoever took them must be a good photographer.

FREDDIE: That can't be an easy job.

S: Forensic photographer?

FREDDIE: Having to look at what no one wants to see. Get close. Focus. Frame. I don't know. I couldn't do it.

S: Must be horrible.

FREDDIE: The first one is really striking. The one you compared to the paintings?

S: Yes, the Saint Sebastian photo. One might even say it's a beautiful photograph.

FREDDIE: What I was saying is I was thinking of the photos and the business about not being able to show them. I don't know. It made me think about how in Greek tragedies they weren't allowed to show violent acts onstage.

S: It's true. I hadn't thought of that. Maybe, when we get to the reenactment, we... Speaking of the Greeks, I was reading Oedipus at Colonus yesterday and found this excerpt. I don't know. When I read it, it reminded me of what you said at your audition. About Oedipus being an unknowing patricide or that he wasn't a bonafide patricide because he does it, he doesn't actually know he's killing his own father. Sophocles made the same claim, in a sense. And what's most noteworthy is that he gives the lines to Oedipus himself. Here. I printed it out. Have a read. Actually, would you mind reading it out loud? The underlined bit.

FREDDIE: *'If I stood up against my father, if I killed him, completely oblivious of what I was doing and oblivious of the identity of my victim, why then am I punished and condemned for a crime I did not intend? If someone on the road approached you suddenly, in an ambush, intending to kill you, would you take the time to find out if your intended assassin is your father before defending yourself, or would you rush to defend yourself and strike him? I am certain that my father's soul would not contradict me if he lived'.*

S: That last sentence is beautiful, right? I am certain that my father's soul would not contradict me if he lived.

FREDDIE: That's deep. It's exactly what I said to you on the day of the audition. Oedipus isn't a one hundred percent patricide.

S: Yeah. But Sophocles put it better than you.

FREDDIE: Really?

S: And he goes further still. What he is saying is that in the end, we all kill our fathers a little without realising it.

FREDDIE: Does he?

S: Yes.

FREDDIE: If you say so. The strangest part for me is how he's always held up as an example of patricide, when really his case is much more confusing and muddled.

S: Well… Exactly. Surely that's the reason why he acts as the perfect paradigm for patricide. We're not about to claim that it isn't a fairly confusing and muddled subject, are we?

FREDDIE: Yes. No. You're right.

S: I don't know. It's like a place where things are never very clear. I think it happens to all of us, kind of. We definitely all have our slightly ambiguous version of Thebes, just like Oedipus. Somewhat dark and confusing. I don't know. A sort of incomprehensible zone or territory. No? A sort of Thebes Land.

FREDDIE: A what?

S: A Thebes Land. Actually that could be the title…

FREDDIE: The title of what?

S: Of this. All of this. Thebes Land.

FREDDIE: Febes Land?

S: With a T H. *Thebes Land.* Yes I like that. Come on. Shall we play a little?

* * *

S: When I got to the hotel that night, a letter had arrived from the prison. It was a letter from Martin in which he apologised. He was apologising again for having been rude. In two brief lines. And on the other side of the letter, he had written a long list of words. It was the list of basketball terms I'd asked him for. I still have it. It's a beautiful list. It's divided into five parts. And Martin named each part after names that are used to designate the five periods that can make up a basketball game. First quarter. Second quarter. Third quarter. Fourth quarter. And Over Time. I read it several times that night. I couldn't help admiring the considerable literary work he had created. Notwithstanding the fact that there was no concern for syntax in the compiling of the list, let alone any observation of proper grammar, or verbs, or anything connecting the words, it was nevertheless evident that Martin had taken the literary care of conjuring up, through language, a whole series of images that were in his mind's eye. And he'd done so in order to transport them to a blank page. Every time I read it I feel the same pleasure I imagine he must have felt in writing it. The pleasure of listing words without any manner of hierarchy and without worrying about any sort of composition. The pleasure of writing without wondering what goes before or after each word. The list is as follows.

FIRST QUARTER. Basketball. Game. Jump ball. Opening tip. Possession. Offence. Half-court. Dribble. Shot. Three-pointer. Brick. Rebound. Putback. Score. Two-points. SECOND QUARTER. Team. Starters. Bench. Coach. Point guard. Shooting guard. Small Forward. Power forward. Centre. Sixthman. Big man. Swingman. Teammate. Opponent. Winner. Loser. THIRD QUARTER. Offense. Drop step. Finger roll. Fadeaway. Run and gun. Downtown. In and out. Fast break. Behind the back. Wrap Around. Alley oop. Slam dunk. FOURTH QUARTER. Defence. Man to man. Zone. Two-three. One-three-one. Full-court press. Foul. Personal foul. Flagrant foul. Technical foul. Holding. Blocking. Charging. Ejection. Elimination. Disqualification. OVER TIME. Showtime. Time of play. Shot clock. Hangtime. Air time. Prayer. Buzzer beater. Time Out. Half Time.

* * *

INTERVAL

THIRD QUARTER

S: I like watching you play.

MARTIN: I know. I can tell.

S: And you like being watched, right?

MARTIN: I told you. It don't bother me.

S: You're good.

MARTIN: I know that, too. *(MARTIN dribbles.)* I can do it from over here, too. Thud.

S: You have good aim.

MARTIN: I'm good at calculating. It's just a matter of being able to calculate distance and velocity. That's all. See? *(MARTIN dribbles.)* Aren't you coming in?

S: Yes.

MARTIN: Do want a go?

S: No. Thank you.

MARTIN: No, thank you. Why won't you try?

S: I'm not very good at ball games.

MARTIN: None of them?

S: They're not really my thing.

MARTIN: What about football?

S: No. I don't play that either.

MARTIN: You don't like football?

S: I'd rather watch it.

MARTIN: Me too. I like playing basketball but I'd rather watch football. Who's your favourite team?

S: I don't have one.

MARTIN: Mine's Man U.

S: Okay. Tottenham. I guess.

MARTIN: Spurs are shit. Manchester United are the best. Well, they were. Who's your favourite player?

S: I don't know. Gareth Bale. Messi.

MARTIN: What about Zidane?

S: Yes. Of course. I like him too.

MARTIN: He's my favourite player.

S: Well… He was very good.

MARTIN: He's the best ever. The best by miles.

S: Maybe.

MARTIN: There's no one else like him.

S: That famous headbutt, right?

MARTIN: The headbutt…

S: Yes. The head butt. *The Materazzi headbutt.*

MARTIN: That's because he cussed him. Materazzi cussed Zidane's sister.

S: Yes. I know.

MARTIN: And his mum.

S: Sometimes I watch it on YouTube.

MARTIN: The headbutt?

S: Just that clip. On repeat. I like watching Zidane hitting Materazzi square in the middle of his chest.

MARTIN: Just like that. Two steps back and one good, hard hit. Bam. Full-on and dead centre. Zidane. Best ever. So you do know a bit about football.

S: No. Very little. Hardly anything.

MARTIN: I read an article the other day. Guess what it was about it? You've got three guesses.

S: Was it about Zidane?

MARTIN: No.

S: I don't know. Messi?

MARTIN: No. One more guess. I'll give you a clue.

S: Basketball?

MARTIN: Yeah. It was an article about you. Well, actually, it was about your dad, how your dad played basketball when he was younger.

S: Ah. Yes. How did you…?

MARTIN: The librarian showed it to me. Cos he knows… Was he a professional?

S: My father?

MARTIN: Yeah. Was he a professional basketball player?

S: Yes. When he was young.

MARTIN: And now?

S: No. He only played for a few years. But that was a while ago. Before I was born. Then he stopped.

MARTIN: And was he good?

S: I don't know. I never saw him play. I think so. He must have been. It never occurred to me to ask him.

MARTIN: Is he dead?

S: Who? My father? No. No. He's alive. I spoke with him this morning.

MARTIN: And do you get on with him?

S: Yes. Generally. We argue a bit sometimes. But we get on.

MARTIN: So… I mean… Do you love him?

S: Yes. Of course. Very much.

MARTIN: And him?

S: What?

MARTIN: Does he love you too?

S: Yes. Of course. Well… I've never asked him that either. But I imagine so. I imagine he loves me very much.

MARTIN: My dad never loved me. I know because he told me. All the time.

S: What did he say?

MARTIN: I don't love you. I don't love you, he said. Any time something happened, any time there was a problem or something, I don't love you anyway. I never loved you. And I'm never going to love you, he'd say. He always wanted to let me know in one way or another. Since I was little. Since I was very little. And sometimes he'd walk past me and hit me just because. Bam. Punch me. Right in the face. And if I complained. Bam. Another punch. I think he enjoyed it.

S: Enjoyed what?

MARTIN: You know. Enjoyed hitting me. It gave him pleasure. He used to hit my mum too. And also just because. Bam. Out of nowhere. Bam. All of a sudden he'd feel like hitting us. Bam. Bam. Bam. Sometimes he'd go and get a belt and whack us hard on our backs.

S: With the belt?

MARTIN: Yes. Right here. This part here. Where it hurts most. And sometimes he'd even do it in front of his friends. He'd sit them on the couch, stand me in front of them and hit me. With everything he had. But the belt was the worst. Cos of the buckle. That really messed you up. Besides, the belt left marks. On the skin. Like sores. And then it would hurt for days. It hurt when I moved, when I showered. Skin too tight. Other times he hits me here. On this part of my neck. Where the vein is. And afterward the pain goes up to my head. Other times he picks up a book and hits me with it. Or he uses them as a vice to crush my hands. My fingers. Inside the book. And then… then he'd stamp on them. That ever happen to you?

S: No.

MARTIN: He did it until my hands were bleeding. Understand? That's why I don't go to the library. It reminds me. It hurts so much. It's like getting your hand caught in a door. My fingernails would turn black. Then, when I started growing, he stopped hitting me. He kept hitting my mum. He hit her until she died. But yeah, with me, he stopped after a while. Well I was his height, you know. But instead of hitting me,

65

he started insulting me. Saying horrible horrible things to me. Then, one day, my mum died. Because she's dead.

S: Yes. I know.

MARTIN: She had cancer. Cancer of the uterus, they said. And then it got worse. My dad started saying mum died because of me. That if she'd never had me, then she wouldn't have got cancer in her uterus and died. Those were the worst years. I wanted to leave home but had nowhere to go. So I had to go out and work. Earn a living. But I weren't good at anything.

S: That can't be true?

MARTIN: Because I was useless, like my dad said. Turned out he was right. And I kept getting sacked from every job. Until, well… One time… One time I prostituted myself. And, well… I was good at that… I was good at it…

S: It's a job like any other.

MARTIN: No. It isn't. That's when my dad started calling me a whore. One of his mates slept with me and went and told my dad. Told my dad I was prostituting myself. The same mate that, when I was little, would come and sit on the couch and watch my dad hit me with his belt. And from that point on… He said that if I used to make him angry, now I made him sick. And then every time he saw me he'd call me a whore. That's the only thing he would call me. Whore. Until one day I couldn't take it anymore and I killed him. One morning. A Sunday. There are photos. Have you seen them?

S: Yes. I saw them.

MARTIN: All of them?

S: Well… I don't know. I saw a few. The ones in the file.

MARTIN: Ah, right. Then you've seen them all. I was shown them loads. Especially when I had to do the reenactment. The reenactment of the crime. Do you know what that is?

S: I didn't know you'd / …

MARTIN: Everything has to be the same. Exactly the same. That's why they show you the photos. They take you to the crime scene. That's what they call it. They take you there and you have to do everything the same. The same things. The same steps. The same movements. You have to do everything the same. One of the officers played my... the... The dead man. The body. And you have to do everything the same. And you have to tell him, the guy who's pretending to be your, what he has to do, what he did. It's weird. It's as if it was the same but not the same. What time is it?

S: It's almost five.

MARTIN: They'll be coming to get me. I've got to go see the medic.

S: Are you ill?

MARTIN: No. I've got to get my medication. Because of the epilepsy. Do you know what that is?

S: Yes. of course.

MARTIN: Well, I've got it. Epilepsy.

S: I know.

MARTIN: Sometimes... My whole body shakes. I see things. My jaw hurts. That's why I have to take these pills all the time. But the only thing that actually calms me down is this rosary. That's why I always have it on me.

S: The rosary your mother gave you?

MARTIN: Well... She didn't exactly give it to me. I kept it after she died. It was hers. It's the only thing of hers I kept. Do you like it?

S: It's very pretty.

MARTIN: Very pretty. You always use words that... I don't know.

S: That's because it is very pretty.

MARTIN: My mum was a good person. She really loved me. And I loved her. There was something between us. You know. We loved each other. We really loved each other. I think my mum actually loved me more than she loved my dad.

S: I think they're coming to get you.

MARTIN: Yeah. Yeah. It's time for you to go. When you coming back?

S: Thursday. Same as always.

MARTIN: Okay. Can I ask you something? Do you think it's possible…?

S: What?

MARTIN: That a mum could die because of the child she had. That the cancer could be her child's fault.

S: No. The two things are completely unrelated.

MARTIN: Right. Right. So see you the day after tomorrow. I'll be here. As usual.

S: Are you going to keep on playing?

MARTIN: Yeah, until they come get me, yeah.

S: You'll be all sweaty.

MARTIN: I don't mind. *(MARTIN dribbles.)*

* * *

S: You're soaking.

FREDDIE: I ran here. I was afraid I'd be late. I got caught in the rain.

S: Relax. It's fine.

FREDDIE: It's just if I miss my bus, then it becomes a nightmare.

S: Do you live far from here?

FREDDIE: About half an hour away. If you run.

S: You're all out of breath.

FREDDIE: Just give me a sec.

S: I sent you a scene last night.

FREDDIE: Yes. It's really good.

S: I sat down and wrote it as soon as I got home.

FREDDIE: Were you inspired?

S: It's just that Martin would not stop talking yesterday. He talked a lot. I don't know. He told me so much all of a sudden. He talked about the crime. His father. His mother. His epilepsy.

FREDDIE: Is he really epileptic?

S: He is, yes.

FREDDIE: I thought you'd made that up. That that was something you came up with.

S: No. No. I wrote everything he said to me yesterday, to the letter. Apparently he suffers epileptic attacks that induce his visions. I wrote down exactly what he said… I don't remember what I wrote.

FREDDIE: You wrote… I see things.

S: That's it. That's what he said. I didn't want to ask too much. But as I was leaving the prison, they introduced me to his doctor who told me a bit about it. He has a kind of acute epilepsy that includes visions. According to the doctors, he must have been epileptic since his teens, but it's only in prison that he's been diagnosed. It seems quite serious. It causes him a lot of suffering, physical and mental. The doctor was telling me that the attacks are usually triggered by specific episodes.

FREDDIE: I swear I thought you'd made it up.

S: No. I guess I could have, but no. He really is epileptic. What I'd like to know more about is the visions.

FREDDIE: Did the doctors not say anything?

S: No. In any case, I'd like him to be the one to tell me. You know, last night, after I'd finished writing, I started searching the internet for anything on visions and the like, I stumbled across the subject of saints and miracles and apparitions. And it occurred me to look up Saint Martin. The saint. Saint Martin of Tours. And I started finding some unbelievable things. Lots of coincidences.

FREDDIE: With the saint?

S: Yes. For example, the conflictive relationship Saint Martin had with his father, who was a Roman soldier and didn't agree with his son converting to Christianity. And then, the visions Saint Martin had all the time. And his withdrawal from others. His retreats at monasteries. So much of it made me think of Martin. But what really struck me was a painting in which Saint Martin appears with a circle of orange fire over his head.

FREDDIE: A circle of fire?

S: It's meant to have been one of his miracles. It seems that, once, while he was giving mass, an orb of fire appeared suddenly above his head. Like an orange ball floating over Saint Martin's head throughout the liturgy. And it's odd because, when you look at the painting, it looks like a basketball. It's amazing, right? Look, I brought you the picture.

FREDDIE: Yes. Really. It looks like a basketball.

S: What do you think it actually was?

FREDDIE: What?

S: That ball of fire that everyone who was at that mass claims to have seen.

FREDDIE: Probably an optical illusion.

S: Some reflection of light. Or something like that. Or maybe it was an actual ball of fire.

FREDDIE: Maybe. Do you believe in miracles?

S: Maybe. Sometimes.

FREDDIE: I don't.

S: You never know.

FREDDIE: Are you religious?

S: Don't take this the wrong way, but I think that's a bit of a personal question.

FREDDIE: Sorry. I'm sorry.

S: No. It's fine.

FREDDIE: I didn't realise that…

S: Don't worry about it. Right, were you able to print the pages I sent you yesterday?

FREDDIE: Yes, I have it here. The bit about the rosary is great.

S: I'd like us to read the last part.

FREDDIE: Right. From which point?

S: Where he asks the time.

FREDDIE: Okay.

S: Ready? Are you off book?

FREDDIE: Yeah. I learnt it last night.

S: Okay.

FREDDIE: What time is it?

S: It's almost five.

MARTIN: They'll be coming to get me. I've got to go see the medic.

S: Are you ill?

MARTIN: No. I've got to get my medication. Because of the epilepsy. Do you know what that is?

S: Yes. Of course.

MARTIN: Well, I've got it. Epilepsy.

S: Yes. I know.

MARTIN: Sometimes… My whole body shakes. I see things. My jaw hurts. That's why I have to take these pills all the time. But the only thing that actually calms me down is my rosary. That's why I always have it on me.

S: Is that the rosary your mother gave you?

MARTIN: Well… She didn't exactly give it to me. I kept it after she died. It was hers. It's the only thing of hers I have. Do you like it?

S: It's very pretty.

MARTIN: Very pretty. You always use words that... I don't know.

S: That's because it is very pretty.

MARTIN: My mother was a good person. She really loved me.

S: Stop... I'd like to add something new there. When he says that the only thing he kept was a rosary, let's add that he also kept a CD. For example, something like... I kept it after she died. It was hers. It's the only thing I kept. That and a CD. A CD she used to listen to all the time. A Whitney Houston CD. She was her favourite singer. And her favourite song was on that CD. *I Have Nothing.* Something like that...

FREDDIE: Just after the bit with the rosary?

S: Yes... It's the only thing of hers I kept. That and a CD. And then talk about the CD, about Whitney Houston, about *I Have Nothing*, and then go back to the rosary so I can ask him if he likes it.

FREDDIE: Oh yeah, the bus?

S: Yes. Ever since, I can't get it out of my head. Besides, I think *I Have Nothing* could really suit this moment. Just when he's talking about the love he has for his mother. You said you knew the song, right?

FREDDIE: Yeah, I love that song. *The Bodyguard* is my all-time favourite film.

S: Great. I brought it. We can listen to it.

FREDDIE: Alright. Actually, as we've stopped, can I ask about the rosary? At one point he says it's made of jasmine.

S: Yes. A rosary made of jasmine petals.

FREDDIE: Wouldn't a rosary made of rose petals be better?

S: So. I had the same thought. I thought rose petals might be a bit feminine. I don't know. Jasmine petals seemed more masculine to me.

FREDDIE: Rose petals are much better. Rosary. Roses.

S: It's bit on the nose. And, I'm worried it might sound a bit gay. Rose petal rosary. The inmate that smells of roses. It's really camp. Suddenly we're in this gay kitsch aesthetic?

FREDDIE: And what's wrong with that?

S: Nothing. It's just… I'll think about it. Here, listen.

FREDDIE: The middle eight is glorious.

S: Okay. So I want to try it with the song playing in the background. Right after… Is that the rosary your mother gave you?

FREDDIE: Well… She didn't exactly give it to me. I kept it after she died. It was hers. It's the only thing of hers I kept. Well, and a CD. Her favourite CD. She used to listen to all the time. A Whitney Houston CD. Do you know her? She was her favourite singer. And her favourite song was on that CD. *I Have Nothing*. But, still, the only thing that really calms me down is her rosary. Do you like it?

S: It's very pretty.

MARTIN: Very pretty. You always use words that… I don't know.

S: That's because it is very pretty.

MARTIN: My mother was a good person. She really loved me. And I loved her. There was something between us. I don't know. We loved each other. We really loved each other. I think my mum actually loved me more than she loved my dad.

S: It's terrible what he says, don't you think? We really loved each other. I think my mum actually loved me more than she loved my dad. It's awful.

FREDDIE: And is that what he said? Just like that?

S: Just like that, yes. I changed a word or two just to make it flow a little better. We really loved each other. I think my mum actually loved me more than she loved my dad. Strange…

FREDDIE: What?

S: You have the exact same trainers he does.

73

FREDDIE: Do I?

S: Yes. Exactly the same design. Same colour.

FREDDIE: Really?

S: They're identical. The same ones.

FREDDIE: Given how much these cost, his are probably fakes.

S: Could be.

FREDDIE: They do make some incredible imitations nowadays. These are originals.

S: Or maybe it's the other way around.

FREDDIE: As in?

S: Maybe yours are the fakes.

FREDDIE: You think so?

S: Why not?

FREDDIE: Can you play the song again?

S: Again?

FREDDIE: Is that alright?

S: Yes. Sure.

FREDDIE: I don't know. I feel like listening to it again.

* * *

S: Do you like it?

MARTIN: She used to play it all the time. She'd play it really loud every time she locked herself in her room. On full volume. So I wouldn't hear her crying. I know the lyrics by heart. I sing it all the time. Like, every day. It's like a sort of my Hail Mary. Do you know the Hail Mary by heart?

S: Yes.

MARTIN: The whole thing?

S: Yes. The whole thing.

MARTIN: Alright, then.

S: What?

MARTIN: Say it.

S: Say what?

MARTIN: The Hail Mary.

S: Hail Mary, full of grace, the Lord is with you, blessed are thou among women and blessed is the fruit of thy womb, Jesus. Holy Mary, mother of God, pray for us sinners, now and at the hour of our death. Amen.

MARTIN: The first part is what the angel says to her. The Angel Gabriel when he comes to tell her she's pregnant.

S: Yes. It's lovely. Blessed is the fruit of thy womb…

MARTIN: So you're a believer, then?

S: Pardon?

MARTIN: You believe in God, yeah?

S: I find that question difficult to answer.

MARTIN: Oh. So. You can ask me if you like?

S: It's not a question I ask.

MARTIN: But you can ask me.

S: Alright… Are you a believer?

MARTIN: Yes. Of course. I believe. I'm a believer. I've always believed. Because I… I see things sometimes. Sometimes I have what they call visions. It's the reason my head starts hurting and I get the attacks.

S: And… What do you see?

MARTIN: Well… Stuff like you see in dreams. But I don't want to talk about that right now.

S: Okay.

MARTIN: Do I have to?

S: What?

MARTIN: I don't know. Talk about it.

S: No. No. You don't have to talk to me about anything. We only talk about what you feel like talking about. Same as always.

MARTIN: And you, what do you feel like talking about?

S: Okay. well, I wanted to tell you that the script I'm writing is coming along.

MARTIN: Have you finished it?

S: No, not yet.

MARTIN: And… am I in it much?

S: Throughout.

MARTIN: And what do I do? Do I talk?

S: Yes. And you play basketball.

MARTIN: Really?

S: Yes. The actor that's playing you, he's been training every morning at a basketball club.

MARTIN: And I'm on stage?

S: Yes. The whole time. You never leave. Not even in the interval. You're the protagonist.

MARTIN: Like a sort of superhero?

S: Yes. More or less.

MARTIN: So I'm a good guy, right? I mean… Because the superhero is always a good guy.

S: You're the protagonist. You're the main character. You're the most important character in the play.

MARTIN: But am I good or not?

S: Yes. You're good.

MARTIN: Okay. Cool.

S: I mean, you're like everyone. Not good or bad. Or good and bad at the same time. I don't know.

MARTIN: But am I mainly good?

S: Yes.

MARTIN: So I don't kill my dad in your play?

S: No. You do.

MARTIN: And I'm still good, even though I kill him?

S: When you see it, you'll understand. Did I tell you I already have the title?

MARTIN: The what?

S: The title. The name of the play. It's called *Thebes Land*.

MARTIN: What?

S: Thebes Land. Land of Thebes.

MARTIN: What's Febes?

S: Thebes is the name of a very famous city. It was an ancient city where the Oedipus myth took place. Have you ever heard of Oedipus?

MARTIN: No. Who is he?

S: Someone who had similar experiences to you.

MARTIN: Did his mum die too?

S: Oedipus is a man who killed his father. No one actually knows for certain whether he actually existed. It's a myth. A story. And Oedipus is the main character of that story.

MARTIN: The superhero?

S: Exactly. He's the hero of the whole story.

MARTIN: And did he go to prison?

S: No. Because his story is different. When he killed his father, he didn't actually know it was his father. Because his parents had abandoned him as a baby. They gave him to someone who hung him by his heels from a tree. That's why his name is Oedipus. It means he of the swollen feet. Then a different person cut him down from the tree, saved his life and took him to another country.

MARTIN: Far from Febes?

S: Yes, to Corinth. That's why when Oedipus is older and returns to Thebes, he kills his father, who is King of Thebes, on the road, not knowing it is his father. And then he marries the Queen of Thebes, not knowing she is his mother.

MARTIN: He marries his mum?

S: Yes.

MARTIN: And sleeps with her?

S: Yes. Of course.

MARTIN: And they have sex?

S: And children.

MARTIN: Together?

S: Yes, together.

MARTIN: Swear down

S: I swear.

MARTIN: And she knew he was her son.

S: No, neither of them had any idea.

MARTIN: So it's not their fault, then.

S: But one day they find out about everything. One day he finds out the man he killed was his father and the woman he's married is his mother.

MARTIN: And what does he do?

S: He tears out his eyes.

MARTIN: Just like that? How?

S: Yes. He goes to the room where his mother's body is, she's hanged herself after finding out, he takes the brooch from her hair and blinds himself with the pin.

MARTIN: And he's blinded?

S: Completely. There are two black holes where his eyes should be.

MARTIN: And then?

S: They throw him out. They banish him. He has to leave.

MARTIN: Leave Thebes?

S: Yes. Leave Thebes.

MARTIN: He leaves…

S: Yes. No one wants him in the city. Haven't you ever heard the story?

MARTIN: Once. No. Maybe. At school… A teacher told us a similar story once. Something about the tragedy of Greece.

S: Yes. That's the one. Because a lot of people wrote about that story afterwards. And many centuries ago in Greece there were people who took that story and wrote plays known as tragedies. There's one called *Oedipus Tyrannos*. Another called *Oedipus at Colonus*.

MARTIN: Yes. It really is a tragedy.

S: Well. That's exactly why I want to call my play Thebes Land. Now do you understand?

MARTIN: But I never slept with my mum.

S: I know that. But, in a way, what happened to you is similar to what happened to Oedipus.

MARTIN: Because of the thing with his dad?

S: Of course. And did you know that every time a person kills their father, the story of Oedipus always comes up.

MARTIN: But he didn't go to prison?

S: No. But he was banished, which was kind of the same thing at the time, maybe worse. It's a great story.

MARTIN: And did they make a film of it?

S: Yes. There's a few films. Pasolini's is my favourite.

MARTIN: And on TV?

S: I don't know. But I don't think so. There are also some paintings.

MARTIN: Please.

S: The paintings?

MARTIN: Yes. I really like looking at paintings.

S: I can get them for you. I'll get pictures of the paintings and I'll bring them.

MARTIN: Nice.

S: And I'll also bring you the two tragedies to read. They might have them in the library.

MARTIN: I don't go to the library. I don't like books. I already told you. Remember?

S: Sorry. I forgot. That's right.

MARTIN: No. It's fine. What did you say he was called?

S: Oedipus.

MARTIN: And his parents?

S: His father was Laius.

MARTIN: And the mother?

S: Jocasta.

MARTIN: Oedipus, Laius and Jocastra.

S: No. Jocasta.

MARTIN: Why are you laughing?

S: Because you made a mistake and it was funny.

MARTIN: I, what?

S: You said Jocastra instead of Jocasta.

MARTIN: Yeah and I misheard you. Why's that funny?

S: Because Jocasta suddenly becomes Jocastra. Which makes us think of castration. As in when they cut off your genitals.

MARTIN: That must be horrible.

S: Castration?

MARTIN: No. Sleeping with your own mum. I keep thinking it must be horrible.

S: Yes. Probably.

MARTIN: Must be why he blinded himself.

S: He does it when he finds out about everything.

MARTIN: Yes, but I think he does it because he slept with his mum. Not so much for killing his dad. Right?

S: Yes. You might be right.

MARTIN: Must be horrible.

S: I have to go.

MARTIN: Already?

S: Yes. It's time.

MARTIN: And... What did he kill him with? His dad... I mean...

S: No one really knows. Some versions say he used a club.

MARTIN: I killed mine with a fork.

S: Yes. I know.

MARTIN: It's getting late.

S: I'll be back the day after tomorrow.

MARTIN: Alright. I'll be here.

* * *

S: Some days later I was summoned by Mehmet and Leyla. We met upstairs. They had received an email from the Ministry of Justice wherein it was expressly forbidden for Martin to attend the performances. The refusal was brief and definitive. The only thing they would authorise, and with many reservations, was for him to attend a dress rehearsal under armed guard with no other audience present. At this stage it was impossible to halt the entire project. Rehearsals were far too along and opening night was upon us.

FREDDIE: So he won't be able to be there.

S: No. He'll only be able to see a rehearsal without an audience. They won't allow him to attend any of the performances. I've managed to get us a direct video feed so Martin can watch every performance from the prison.

FREDDIE: Will everything be filmed?

S: The entire time. In fact, if we're going to create a live video feed, we could show it at any prison that was interested.

FREDDIE: I like that.

S: Hence the camera. Besides, I find it interesting from a theatrical point of view. Being seen live by people we can't see. Like inmates. It's a bit strange, isn't it?

FREDDIE: Yes.

S: I don't know if you saw that I've been working on the crime scene re-enactment bit / Did you get the crime scene reenactment I sent you at the end of last week?

FREDDIE: Yeah. I did. It's amazing. It went in. Really easy. This process of making him reenact the crime is pretty haunting, isn't it?

S: Yes. It was hard listening to him explain how they took him back home and made him do it. Made him relive it. Perform the same actions. Kill his father again.

FREDDIE: Must have been terrible.

S: Very… Very theatrical.

FREDDIE: But then he wanted to reenact for you as well?

S: Yes. The other day. It was truly… violent. I told him he didn't have to. But he insisted, that he had to show me. I didn't want him to do it. I had no desire to see him playing out the scene of the murder there, in front of me. I knew it would shock me. That I would feel uncomfortable. And I did. It was shocking.

FREDDIE: And he just acted it out exactly like it happened?

S: He stood before me and, carefully minding each movement, played the whole scene, step by step. It was like being made to witness something you really don't want to see. He was explaining every action with utter precision. Every gesture. He stood before me, like this, and started. It was a Sunday… Early morning… Very early… That's how he started and he didn't stop until he'd told me everything. It was horrible. Seeing him repeat the same actions. The same movements. It's all there.

FREDDIE: Do you want me to…?

S: I don't know.

* * *

MARTIN / FREDDIE: It was a Sunday. Early morning. Very
early. I walk in. I open the door and walk in. He's in
the kitchen. There. He'd gotten up to get a glass of
water. Suddenly he looks at me and says can't you even
remember to bring home a pint of milk. Just because. And
that's when I say if he wants milk he should go and get
it himself. You're a whore, he says. I don't answer. Did
you hear me? he says. I still don't answer. So then he calls
me a whore again. See? I'm calling you a whore and you
won't even defend yourself. Whore. And that's when it
happens. That's when I have the vision. That's when I see
the apparition. Like in the Hail Mary. It's the same. The
apparition is there. In front of me. And it gestures to me.
With its arm. Like this. So I go to the cutlery drawer and
open it. Whore. You whore. I choose a fork. I don't say
anything. I don't talk. Whore, he says again. I turn around.
I move towards him. I raise the fork and stab him with it.
Like this. In one blow. In the neck. One. What are you
doing?, he shouts at me. He tries to stop me, but I push
him. Against the refrigerator. And then I stab him again.
Two. In the same spot. Always in the same spot. In the
neck. You're crazy, he shouts at me. You're hurting me.
Then I stab him a third time, slightly further down. Here.
Three. And then he screams even louder. But, what are
you doing? You're hurting me. Can't you see?, he says,
can't you see you're a whore, a whore you can't even
remember to buy a pint of milk? That's when he tries to
push me again, but I jam him with my right leg and that's
when I stab him a fourth time. In the throat. Like this.
Right in the throat. Four. You're killing me, he screams.
And then I stick it all the way in. As deep as possible so
he'll stop talking. So he can't talk anymore. You're killing
your own father, he says. Then I stab him a couple of times
right in the throat. Five. Six. And that's when the blood
starts going everywhere. His neck starts opening up. He
wants to say something, but the only thing coming out of
his throat are noises. Like snores mixed with the blood.
Then I carry on stabbing him with the fork a couple more
times. Seven. Eight. To kill him completely. So he'll shut

up. I stab him here. Behind the ear. Nine. And here, under the jaw. Ten. And here. Eleven. And I also stab him in the chest. Twelve. And here, where the liver is. Thirteen. And on this side, too. Fourteen. And then here, right in the belly. Fifteen. And then in this part of the groin. Right here. Sixteen. And then there. In the crotch. Seventeen. Again. Eighteen. Nineteen. Twenty. Twenty one. That's when I realised he was dead. His eyes were open, but he wasn't actually breathing anymore. It seemed like he was still looking at me. That even though he was dead he was still looking at me the same way. Dad, I said. Dad. Dad. But he didn't answer. He was dead. He was completely dead.

S: Enough. Let's stop there. That's enough for today.

* * *

MARTIN: Why won't you come in?

S: How are you?

MARTIN: Alright…

S: Did they tell you?

MARTIN: Yesterday.

S: It's out of our hands.

MARTIN: I know.

S: I'm sorry.

MARTIN: I wanted to go. I wanted to be there.

S: You'll still be present throughout. Everyone will hear your story. The real one.

MARTIN: Yes. I know. But I wanted to be able to go. Because I never see anyone here. No one ever comes. I've got no one to come visit me. What I wanted was to be able to go to the theatre.

S: I wanted you to come, too.

MARTIN: To get out for a bit.

S: You'll still be able to come to a rehearsal. That's already been approved.

MARTIN: But I won't be able to go every night.

S: There will be a broadcasting system. You'll be able to see every performance. That's also been approved.

MARTIN: Yeah. They explained. But it won't be the same.

S: Many more people will get to know your story.

MARTIN: I'm gonna be a star.

S: In a manner of speaking. Do you want to play?

MARTIN: No. I don't feel like it.

S: We could also try to get an internet connection. For Skype. We could arrange to have a conversation during the performance. Or after.

MARTIN: Yes, but I wanted to get out for a bit.

S: Well… That's exactly what they don't want.

MARTIN: Because I won't ever be able to go outside again.

S: Sometimes…

MARTIN: Not in my case. It's forever for me. I'm gonna be locked in here forever. Forever and ever and ever. Till the day I die.

S: Sometimes lawyers…

MARTIN: I haven't got any lawyers.

S: Yes. You do. Everyone has a right to an attorney.

MARTIN: Not me. I ain't got money. Or anyone to care about me. There was some solicitor that saw me two or three times. That's it.

S: Maybe I can help.

MARTIN: No. You can't. I'll be in here forever.

S: What is that?

MARTIN: Nothing. Nothing.

S: Why are you hiding it?

MARTIN: It's nothing.

S: What is it?

MARTIN: I told you it's nothing.

S: It's a fork…

MARTIN: So?

S: Nothing. I'm just saying it's a fork.

MARTIN: Does it scare you?

S: What?

MARTIN: Seeing me with a fork.

S: No.

MARTIN: I always have it on me. Right here. Hidden. Just in case.

S: And they let you?

MARTIN: No. They don't know about it.

S: What's wrong?

MARTIN: Nothing.

S: You have blood on your hands.

MARTIN: No.

S: Yes. Yes. What did you do? Did you hurt yourself?

MARTIN: No. It's fine.

S: Do you want me to call someone?

MARTIN: No.

S: What happened?

MARTIN: Nothing. It's nothing.

S: You're hurt.

MARTIN: I think…

S: What's the matter?

MARTIN: Nothing.

S: Are you feeling alright?

MARTIN: I don't know… Suddenly…

S: Do you want me to call someone?

MARTIN: No... I'm a little tired... And the heat... The sun...
   That's all...

S: Why don't we call someone?

MARTIN: It'll pass... It's the light... The sun... The light...

S: You're bleeding.

MARTIN: It was an accident...

S: I need some help.

MARTIN: I think... No... It's... Must be...

S: Martin was beginning to have an attack. They came
   immediately to treat him and I was told to leave. That it
   would be best if I went. I waited a while to get news, but
   they told me there was no use in waiting. That they would
   take him to the infirmary and the doctor would take care of
   him there. I asked the prison doctor to keep me updated.
   When I got back, I had a message from him saying Martin
   had had a severe epileptic fit and that it would be best
   to suspend our meetings for a week until he was better. I
   found it very difficult to sleep that night. I couldn't get the
   image of Martin bleeding with the fork in his hand and
   shaking more and more violently out of my head. I had to
   take a sleeping pill.

* * *

FOURTH QUARTER

S: The day following the attack, I decided that, as I would no longer be able to go to the prison, we would make the most of it and step it up in rehearsals. Opening night wasn't far away. Today, for example, could you stay until seven?

FREDDIE: Yes. Course.

S: Good. In that case we can carry on with the photos a little longer. Look… His head is covered in this one. They're taking him to trial. They always cover their heads.

FREDDIE: What is it?

S: I don't know. I can't tell. Is it a jacket or…

FREDDIE: Isn't it a towel?

S: A towel? Yes. You're right. It's a towel. I think that photo is from the day of the sentencing. The date must be at the bottom.

FREDDIE: I can't make it out.

S: No.

FREDDIE: Has he ever spoken to you about the trial?

S: No. Never. I haven't asked him about it much. I only read the final verdict. The summary judgement, where he is given multiple life sentences.

FREDDIE: It must be terrible knowing the rest of your life… I don't know.

S: You know, the more I know him, the more I understand him killing his father. It's not that he's justifying it. But the more I talk to him, the more explanations I find for what he did. The other day he said… What was it? Ah, yes. Until one day I couldn't stand it anymore and I killed him. And I understand it, you know? The father was a beast. A monster. He beat him all the time. Tortured him. Even in public. Constantly humiliated him. Tore his life apart. His and his mother's too. It's kind of logical that he would have killed him eventually. That he would have put a stop to his ongoing ordeal one day. You know. More than a murder, I wonder if it wasn't actually a legitimate act of self defence. Sometimes I even wonder whether he's a proper patricide.

FREDDIE: But, unlike Oedipus, he knew he was killing his own father.

S: But that's not the reason I say that in his case. I wonder whether he's a patricide, because I don't know if such a monster can be called a father. I don't know. To me, a beast like that isn't really a true father.

FREDDIE: You're getting that Stockholm syndrome.

S: You think so?

FREDDIE: You know how hostages develop sympathy for their captors through familiarity.

S: Could be. But I think it's likelier I've been slightly influenced by what Dostoyevsky says in *The Brothers Karamazov*. Have you /

FREDDIE: I haven't read it.

S: No? You should. It's a remarkable treatise on patricide. I passed a bookshop the other night and bought a copy.

FREDDIE: Is it the first time you've read it?

S: No. No. I was fourteen the first time.

FREDDIE: And did you understand it?

S: Very little. But then I read it again when I was older.

FREDDIE: I remember a teacher always used to tell us it was a literary cathedral.

S: Yes. It's true. In a sense. I was rereading some of it last night. Some passages from the end of the novel. And I wanted to read you one that deals with Old Karamazov, a monstrous character, does he or doesn't he deserve to be treated like a true father.

FREDDIE: Old Karamazov is the father they murder, right?

S: Of course. He's the father of the four brothers.

FREDDIE: Aren't there three?

S: No. I thought you hadn't…

FREDDIE: Some guy on *Mastermind* last week, his specialist / subject…

S: There are four. Look. Here it is. Listen. *'An unjust and hateful father stirs up painful questions in his son, for example: "Did my father love me when he conceived me? If he did not even know me in that moment of passion and may even have been emboldened by alcohol, why, then, must I love him? Merely because he conceived me?" That son ought to ask his father: "Why must I love you? Prove to me that it is a duty." And if the detestable father is unable to prove that his son must love him, the son is then free and has the right to consider the author of his days a stranger or even an enemy. Certain crimes cannot be called patricides. The deaths of certain fathers can only be considered patricides by those blinded by prejudice'.* Shocking, isn't it?

FREDDIE: Yes. It's sort of what you were just saying.

S: He used to crush his hands with books. I don't know if you can call that a father.

FREDDIE: He was also an epileptic, right?

S: Who? The father?

FREDDIE: No. Dostoyevski.

S: Oh. Yes. In fact, he apparently had his first epileptic fit the day after his father's death.

FREDDIE: Wow.

S: A father who had been a tyrant to Dostoyevski, by the way. An alcoholic that made his teenage years impossible.

FREDDIE: A sort of Old Karamazov?

S: Yes. more or less. They say he died a horrible death.

FREDDIE: Who?

S: Dostoyevski's father. He died at the hands of his own slaves after they had tortured him. And it was there, when Dostoyevski learned of it, that he is meant to have had his first attack. What's interesting is that he had wished so much for his father's death that he ended up feeling responsible for the crime for the rest of his life.

FREDDIE: They say they're horrible.

S: What?

FREDDIE: Epileptic fits.

S: Yes. Yes. They say they can be devastating. The convulsions can last several minutes. And the worst part is that they come suddenly, unpredictably. They say it's a real torment. The muscular contractions. The biting one's own tongue. The incontinence. The blows. The loss of consciousness. It seems there are some fits, I mean, episodes, you should say episodes, when the person loses all control. And the tiredness. The tiredness that follows. They say that's the worst part. The person is left completely exhausted. Here. You can keep it.

FREDDIE: No. It's fine. I'll buy my own copy.

S: It's a gift. Take it. I'm giving it to you.

FREDDIE: Alright. Thank you.

S: That way, every time you think of the Karamazovs, you'll remember me.

FREDDIE: Course. I'm still thinking about what you said. That he would crush his hands in books.

S: Horrible, right?

FREDDIE: It would never have occurred to me. Using a book.

S: It's awful. I don't know. Using a book in that way. It's disgusting. It's abhorrent. Perhaps that's the reason he killed him with a fork. He didn't stab him with a knife. He did it with an object that wasn't made for cutting. In a sense, he reverted to the same principle his father used when torturing him. The misuse of an object. Did you see the photos of the fork?

FREDDIE: Yes. I was looking at them.

S: They're odd, right?

FREDDIE: They're unpleasant, more than anything. How it's bent.

S: For me it's the blood. How the prongs are all covered in blood. And the blood's dried. Coagulated.

FREDDIE: I don't know why, but I find these photos more upsetting than those of the body.

S: Yes. I think you're right. And at the same time... There's something... I don't know. The fork inside the plastic bag... It's like an installation at a modern art museum. Like it's been designed, thought up, don't you think? I don't know. There's something poetic about it. I don't know. A fork for a dagger. There's a sort of displacement I find interesting.

FREDDIE: The stains are shocking.

S: It's strange because, remember that peach smoothie he made, well, he washed everything he'd used to make it. The chopping board. The plate. The blender. The glass when he finished. But he didn't wash the fork. He cleaned everything except the murder weapon.

FREDDIE: While his father lay dead beside him?

S: He was alone with the body for several hours, yes.

FREDDIE: I have a question... When these kinds of crimes happen between relatives... I don't know... I imagine the killer is caught almost immediately...

S: Yes. Of course. Martin was arrested that same afternoon.

FREDDIE: And, what about the funeral and everything?

S: Sorry, I don't understand.

FREDDIE: Okay. What I... When it's someone in the family, can the killer go to the funeral?

S: I don't know. I would imagine not.

FREDDIE: So he's never been to see his father's grave?

S: I don't know. It's a good question.

FREDDIE: What happens if the killer asks to go to the funeral or if they ask to see their victim's grave later on?

S: We're getting distracted... Can we, where did we leave off?

FREDDIE: We've just got to the part where Martin is putting his eyedrops in.

S: That's right. Oh… I was thinking… I don't know. Perhaps it would be better if he didn't put the eyedrops in himself.

FREDDIE: Maybe. Perhaps I could ask you to do it.

S: Exactly. Let's give it a go.

FREDDIE: Great.

S: Perhaps it's the only time in the play there's physical contact between them.

FREDDIE: Cool.

S: Let's go back a bit.

FREDDIE: From the top of the scene?

S: Okay.

FREDDIE: I imagine him sort of… Tired… Exhausted… As if he'd given his all after the epileptic fit… I don't know… I imagine him on the stool, totally spent…

* * *

S: Are you better?

MARTIN: Yes. Now I am.

S: Aren't you going to practise today?

MARTIN: No. The doctor said it would be best if I rest.

S: I called every day to ask how you were doing.

MARTIN: I know.

S: If you're too tired, we can do this another day.

MARTIN: No.

S: I can come back tomorrow or the day after.

MARTIN: No. It's fine.

S: The doctor said it was a particularly severe attack.

MARTIN: Yes. The first convulsions lasted a long time. But I'm fine now.

S: Are you in pain?

MARTIN: No. I'm just a bit tired. My whole body. But only a bit. And the light. The light hurts a bit. My eyes.

S: Would you rather go inside?

MARTIN: No. A bit of air will do me good.

S: Okay.

MARTIN: I have to put these drops in, three times a day. What time is it?

S: Five.

MARTIN: So… Let's see…

S: Do you want me to help?

MARTIN: Do you know how?

S: Yes. Give them here.

MARTIN: It's three drops in each eye.

S: Don't worry.

MARTIN: You have to squeeze… They have to land inside the eye.

S: One.

MARTIN: Stop…

S: Don't be frightened. One. Two. Three. Does it sting?

MARTIN: A bit. Now the other one.

S: Let's see… One. Two. Three.

MARTIN: No.

S: The last one landed outside. Let's try again. Right. Three. There you go.

MARTIN: It stings a bit.

S: All done. What exactly is it you have?

MARTIN: With the attacks, sometimes my pupils dilate too much and then I can't see well. And the light hurts. But then it passes.

S: Do you know, the actor playing you has the exact same trainers as you.

MARTIN: Mine are fake. They aren't real.

S: Still, they're very similar.

MARTIN: Maybe. But mine aren't proper. They look real, but they aren't.

S: They do make some incredible imitations now days.

MARTIN: Yeah

S: Does it hurt?

MARTIN: A bit. They sting.

S: I've got to go.

MARTIN: Okay.

S: I promised the governor I was only coming to say hello. To see how you were.

MARTIN: Okay.

S: You need to rest.

MARTIN: Yes. I know.

S: But I'll be back the day after tomorrow. Oh… Do you know, yesterday, while I was working, I came across a phrase and thought of you. It's a phrase by a very famous man called Freud. He was someone who wrote a lot about all the things I told you the other day about Oedipus. And at one point he says something like we all want to kill our fathers. Well… I don't know… When I read it, I thought of you. What he says is kind of true, isn't it? In the end, we all want to, kind of…

MARTIN: You too?

S: Yes. Sure. It's possible that I also wanted to, at some point… I almost forgot… I brought my mp3 player to lend you for a couple days.

MARTIN: How did you?

S: It's okay. So you can listen to a bit of music. It has one particular song I listen to whenever I'm not feeling well.

MARTIN: What is it?

S: It's a piano concerto. Here. Listen.

MARTIN: It's very…

S: Do you like it?

MARTIN: Yes.

S: It's very soothing. I listen to it often.

MARTIN: They're violins…

S: Now comes the piano. You'll see. There.

MARTIN: Ah… Yes… I can hear it now… Why don't you stay a bit longer?

S: I can't.

MARTIN: Just a few minutes…

S: I have to go.

MARTIN: Okay. Close the door properly behind you. Otherwise the wind will slam it and it gets on my nerves.

S: Yes. Of course. Well. See you.

* * *

FREDDIE: It really is extraordinary. It's Mozart, isn't it?

S: I'm impressed.

FREDDIE: I have been known to listen to classical music.

S: Like you've been known to read the classics.

FREDDIE: *(Sighs.)* What is it then?

S: It's his *Piano Concerto N° 21 in C major.* The second movement. The andante.

FREDDIE: And did Martin like it?

S: Very much.

FREDDIE: So that's what he says…

S: Who?

FREDDIE: Freud. That business about all of us kind of wanting to kill our fathers.

S: Yes. And when I told him, he asked me if I felt the same way.

FREDDIE: And what did you say?

S: The truth. That I did. Haven't you ever felt that way?

FREDDIE: Yes. I think so.

S: Do you think it happens to everyone? That we've all got a Thebes Land. You know, that place, that state, where killing your father becomes, I don't know, a real possibility, a thing.

FREDDIE: The tone of the movement is…

S: Slightly sad? He composed it shortly before his father's death. They had fallen out around that time. They weren't speaking. Another pair with a tormented relationship.

FREDDIE: Not another one.

S: Another abusive father. There are even those who say that Mozart's disorders were his fault. But at the same time, maybe, you know, he wouldn't have been the same composer without his father.

FREDDIE: Maybe he would've.

S: The thing is… It shocked me to see him so weak. So fragile. It's strange because I feel guilty about his attack.

FREDDIE: His epileptic f… episode?

S: I don't know. I have the feeling that our recent meetings haven't been doing him any good. Telling him Oedipus's story, for example.

FREDDIE: Hadn't he ever heard it?

S: No. He said they'd spoken about it at school once. I don't think he'd ever properly paid attention to it. I don't know. And also some of the things he told me. Several details. I don't think it did him any good. It's as if, as we've gone on, he's started reliving all of it.

FREDDIE: It's possible. Have you seen the posters?

S: Yes. I saw them this morning. It's like looking into a mirror.

FREDDIE: They're good.

S: Yes. Faces sell. Apparently.

FREDDIE: But do we open on Tuesday the 29th or Wednesday the 30th?

S: So next Tuesday is just for Martin.

FREDDIE: So I get to meet Martin?

S: Yes, and then we start previews officially on Wednesday. And press night is the Monday of the second week.

FREDDIE: So the comps are for Monday.

S: Yes. But if you've got friends who want to see it for cheap, then the first week is all previews.

FREDDIE: Okay.

S: I can give you my comps for Monday, if you like.

FREDDIE: Aren't you going to invite anyone?

S: Just my dad so I only need the one. I can give you the others.

FREDDIE: Well... Yes. Thank you.

* * *

MARTIN: I feel much better today. Much better.

S: I can tell.

MARTIN: It's thanks to the medication. I wasn't well the other day. But I'm much better now. Yesterday I listened to all the music you brought me.

S: Did it help?

MARTIN: I don't know. But I like it.

S: Then it did help.

MARTIN: I can't get it out of my head now. I hear it all the time in here.

S: I'm glad.

MARTIN: And this morning I read what you said in the paper.

S: The interview?

MARTIN: Yes. There's loads of things I didn't understand properly. Loads of difficult words. But I saw you talked about coming in here.

S: The journalist asked me a lot of questions about you.

MARTIN: And about my parents.

S: He wanted to interview you.

MARTIN: If he wants to…

S: But they won't let him. The governor told us it wasn't possible.

MARTIN: Oh… They don't want me to. Better. I'd actually prefer not to. It's better that way. I didn't know you lived in Paris.

S: Yes. I have. I do. Sometimes.

MARTIN: And do you like it?

S: Yes. Very much.

MARTIN: So you speak French.

S: Yes. Of course.

MARTIN: Say something in French.

S: Everyone always… I don't like speaking in French when I'm speaking English.

MARTIN: But do you speak it or not?

S: Yes. I already told you I do.

MARTIN: So say something in French. Please.

S: Okay. What would you like me to say?

MARTIN: I don't know. Let me think… The Lord's Prayer, for example.

S: The Lord's Prayer?

MARTIN: Yes. In French. Our father...

S: Notre Père, qui es aux Cieux, que ton nom soit sanctifié, que ton règne vienne, que ta volonté soit faite sur la terre comme au ciel. Donne-nous aujourd'hui notre pain de ce jour, pardonne-nous nos offenses comme nous pardonnons aussi à ceux qui nous ont offensés et ne nous soumets pas à la tentation, mais délivre-nous du mal. Amen.

MARTIN: Sick. And have you always spoken French?

S: Yes. Since I was very young. But it isn't my mother tongue. My mother tongue is English.

MARTIN: Your mother what?

S: My mother tongue. The first language I learned. The first language one learns is known as one's mother tongue. In my case, for example, French is not my mother tongue.

MARTIN: It's your father tongue.

S: Well... Yes, if you like. In a manner of speaking...

MARTIN: But you don't write in French.

S: No. I always write in English.

MARTIN: Why?

S: I don't know.

MARTIN: Must be because one always writes in one's mother tongue.

S: Well, Yes. Perhaps. Though, there are those who write beautifully in their second language. Nabokov. Beckett.

MARTIN: But you've never wrote in your father tongue.

S: No. Never.

MARTIN: So there's no french in this play you're writing, either?

S: God, no. None whatsoever.

MARTIN: That's good. That way I can understand it. I think I'd also prefer my mother tongue if I were an artist like you. Oh... I wanted to ask you a question, too. What's a contemporary artist?

S: A contemporary artist?

MARTIN: Yes. In the interview, the journalist keeps saying the contemporary artist this… The contemporary artist that…

S: A contemporary artist is… An artist that is alive and dedicated to creating new forms. Forms that didn't exist before. Do you understand? It's what I'm trying to be. The world will be my judge, I guess. It's someone who takes risks at the same time as they're creating something.

MARTIN: Oh right.

S: I don't know if that was clear.

MARTIN: Yes. It was.

S: In any case, I'm glad you read the interview.

MARTIN: Me too.

S: And did you see what was on the next page?

MARTIN: The thing about Messi's tax fraud?

S: No. Before that. There's an article about the discovery of a planet with four suns.

MARTIN: No.

S: Two astronomers have discovered a planet five thousand light years from Earth that is illuminated by four suns. Strange, isn't it?

MARTIN: Yes, I guess…

S: Are you a bit…

MARTIN: What?

S: I don't know. A bit nervous.

MARTIN: No. I'm not.

S: What's the matter?

MARTIN: Nothing.

S: Yes. Something's the matter.

MARTIN: No. Nothing's the matter.

S: Why are you lying to me?

MARTIN: Well… I don't know… Just now…

S: What?

MARTIN: The way you looked at me…

S: What's wrong?

MARTIN: You looked at me… I don't know…

S: I looked at you how?

MARTIN: I don't know… Strangely…

S: I looked at you as I always do.

MARTIN: No. No. You looked at me differently.

S: How?

MARTIN: You. You just looked at… My crotch.

S: Excuse me?

MARTIN: Just now… You looked at my crotch several times.

S: What are you talking about?

MARTIN: That. You looked at me several times. Here. My crotch.

S: Okay. It's possible. But…

MARTIN: You… You like men, right?

S: What?

MARTIN: I asked if you like men?

S: I'm not going to answer that question.

MARTIN: What's wrong with it?

S: It's not that there's anything wrong with it…

MARTIN: So?

S: It's just that it's not relevant.

MARTIN: Well you asked me lots of questions. And I always answered, right?

S: Yes. But…

MARTIN: And besides, I don't see what's wrong with my question. So?

S: Well. Yes. I like some men.

MARTIN: And women? Do you like women?

S: Yes. I like some women.

MARTIN: But you don't sleep with women. That's what I mean.

S: I don't know why you're asking all these questions all of a sudden.

MARTIN: Do you sleep with them or not?

S: What is it that you want to know?

MARTIN: Me, for example, do you like me?

S: Ah... That's what you want to know.

MARTIN: Would you sleep with me, for example?

S: I don't know. I really don't understand why you're so interested...

MARTIN: Why don't you want to answer?

S: And you... Do you like men?

MARTIN: Yes.

S: And women?

MARTIN: Them too. Very much.

S: I don't know why we're talking about this.

MARTIN: You didn't say whether you would sleep with me.

S: Why do you want to know?

MARTIN: Because.

S: No. I don't. No. I mean I don't know. I'm not saying that I wouldn't. I'm not saying I would. I don't know.

MARTIN: Yes. You do. You always know if you would sleep with the person in front of you.

S: No. Not always.

MARTIN: Yes. Always. You know. The problem is you wouldn't have the balls to do it.

S: And why not?

MARTIN: You'd be scared.

S: And what do you know?

MARTIN: I know.

S: And you?

MARTIN: What?

S: Would you?

MARTIN: Sleep with you? Yes. Why not? And I'd ask you to talk to me in French.

S: I think we're done for today.

MARTIN: Are you going?

S: Yes. Yes.

MARTIN: Did my questions bother you?

S: It's just I'm not used to talking about those things.

MARTIN: And my rosary, too…

S: What?

MARTIN: I don't know. You were looking at it funny the whole time. Can you make out the smell of roses?

S: What?

MARTIN: Roses. I told you the other day. It's made of rose petals.

S: Ah, yes. That's right. Yes. Yes. You can smell it from here.

MARTIN: This is yours. Here. It's your mp3 player. I'm returning it.

S: Don't you want to keep it?

MARTIN: No. You lent it to me and I like to return things that I've borrowed.

S: Well… As you wish.

MARTIN: Before you go, can I ask a favour?

S: Yes. Of course.

MARTIN: I need to ask the governor for something. It's important. And if I ask, they'll say no. On the other hand, if you ask, then maybe…

S: Depends on what you want.

MARTIN: I… I'd really like to visit my dad's grave.

S: Okay.

MARTIN: Yes. Because I don't know where it is. No one ever took me.

S: And you want to go?

MARTIN: Yes. Do you think they'll let me?

S: We can try. I'll talk to the governor.

MARTIN: I don't know. Suddenly… I felt like going to see it. They'll probably say no.

S: You never know.

MARTIN: You have to tell them I only want to see the grave. Where it is.

S: I'll talk to them right now…

MARTIN: Please.

S: It's no trouble. And when I come back the day after tomorrow, I'll let you know what they said.

* * *

S: Of course, I knew they'd say no. Still, I tried. I spoke with the governor three times, once in the prison just before I left and twice on the phone. I tried to explain how important the request was. How important it was for Martin to visit his father's grave. The governor couldn't understand why Martin would want to see the grave of the father that he himself had killed in such a horrific fashion. He couldn't see the sense of it. Nor the reason. I told him, I had to tell him twice, three times maybe, that it was something we couldn't know and that, what's more, it was something very personal and perhaps Martin didn't know how to explain. Finally, just when I was about to end the second call, after a long silence, the governor said to me that if Martin wanted to see his father's grave, he would have to choose between the two: either he could come to the theatre or go to the cemetery. But not both. He didn't have the authority. That allowing one excursion had been complicated enough. That inmates only had permission to leave the prison to go to trial or to the hospital in case of serious health problems. Let him choose where he'd prefer to go, he told me before we said our goodbyes. The whole journey back to the hotel I thought the choice would not be an easy one. The cemetery or the theatre. The theatre or the cemetery?

* * *

FREDDIE: And he chose just like that?

S: Instantly. No sooner than I had proposed both options. He didn't hesitate for a second. I told him to think about it but he told me there was nothing to think about. That he was certain. That that was what he wanted.

FREDDIE: How strange?

S: Yes. But at the same time.

FREDDIE: What would you have chosen?

S: Who knows? But given the choice between seeing my father's grave or a play about me... I guess... I think I would've chosen the play.

FREDDIE: I don't know.

S: Both choices are a bit phantasmagorical, don't you think?

FREDDIE: So he didn't hesitate?

S: Just like... *(Clicks fingers.)*

FREDDIE: It's incredible.

S: What?

FREDDIE: I don't know. Human nature. It's something utterly unexpected. Inexplicable. Unfathomable.

S: You've started *The Brothers Karamazov*.

FREDDIE: Yes. Three days ago.

S: I can tell.

FREDDIE: How?

S: The words you just used. The side effects of Dostoyevski are always immediate.

FREDDIE: Yeah, alright.

S: So. Have you tried your costume on?

FREDDIE: Yes.

S: Do you like it?

FREDDIE: Yes. Yes.

S: Does it feel comfortable?

FREDDIE: Yes. Very comfortable.

S: Good. Then we can get started…

FREDDIE: Just…

S: Yes?

FREDDIE: I wanted to thank you.

S: For what?

FREDDIE: I don't know. All of this. For choosing me. Us working together. I don't know. This is for you.

S: What is it?

FREDDIE: It's a gift.

S: Thank you.

FREDDIE: It's a keepsake.

S: I know what it is. It's a rosary.

FREDDIE: Yes. I asked Jemima where she'd bought mine and I got you the same one.

S: Thank you.

FREDDIE: Do you like it?

S: Very much. It's jasmine.

FREDDIE: Yes. Mine too.

S: Oh… Yours too? I don't know. Since you told me a rosary made of roses would be better, I changed it in the script.

FREDDIE: Yes, but in the end I think it's better that it's made of jasmine petals. You were right. It's more masculine.

S: In any case, thank you.

FREDDIE: I liked the idea of giving you a rosary.

S: *(He puts it on.)* So, yesterday I was looking up the origin of your name and do you know what it means?

FREDDIE: No.

S: Peace. Peacemaker. It's of Germanic origin. He that governs for peace.

FREDDIE: I didn't know.

S: I looked it up yesterday. Funny, isn't it? That Martin's war and you're peace.

FREDDIE: And yours? Your name. What does it mean?

S: Mine? Guardian. Guardian or protector.

FREDDIE: Nice!

S: Well, shall we get started?

FREDDIE: The final scene?

S: Yes. The farewell. Oh… One important thing. Right at the end…

FREDDIE: When he looks at him?

S: Yes. Right then. At that moment, just as the lights are fading, Mozart's concerto will be gradually replaced by *Blue Blood* by Foals.

FREDDIE: So you liked it?

S: That bit where the music lifts, it's sort of perfect for when we reach the blackout.

FREDDIE: Great.

S: Shall we?

FREDDIE: Let's.

S: Whenever you're ready.

* * *

OVER TIME

MARTIN: Is that for me?

S: Yes. It's a gift.

MARTIN: Why?

S: To thank you for all your help. And besides, I felt like giving you something.

MARTIN: Do they know about it? Did they let you?

S: Yes. Don't worry. It's all taken care of.

MARTIN: What is it?

S: Open it.

MARTIN: I don't know. It's a bit weird. I'm not used to opening presents.

S: Well... You just rip the paper and that's it.

MARTIN: What is it?

S: Can't you tell?

MARTIN: It's a... A tablet.

S: Yes.

MARTIN: But it's an expensive present.

S: That doesn't matter.

MARTIN: And it's for me?

S: Yes. I'm giving it to you, aren't I?

MARTIN: It's all new.

S: I had to open it because... I've downloaded hundreds of digital books onto it. The classics mainly. The Greeks. The French. The Russians. Dostoyevsky. In English obviously. Some new books too. Things that I've liked. You'll be able to read as much as you like. It'll last you a while.

MARTIN: It's amazing.

S: And I also uploaded lots of the images we looked at.

MARTIN: The paintings?

S: Yes. And an interactive guide to the National Gallery. And the Louvre. That's a museum in Paris. And there's also an encyclopaedia. And I also uploaded Mozart's concertos. The composer you liked. Remember?

MARTIN: Yes. The one that was good for me.

S: That's the one. And I uploaded a bunch of Whitney Houston albums.

MARTIN: Really? Is *I Have Nothing* on there?

S: Yes. Of course. There are two or three versions on there.

MARTIN: And is the play on there?

S: Yes. *Oedipus Tyrannus* is on there.

MARTIN: No. I meant your play.

S: This play?

MARTIN: Yes. Is it on there?

S: Yes. The final draft is, yes. And I've talked to the governor and they'll help you upload newspapers too. Anything you like actually.

MARTIN: I read some of the reviews.

S: Did you see they're talking about you?

MARTIN: Yes. Yes. And the play. They talk a lot about the play.

S: It closes next week.

MARTIN: Already?

S: Well... A month is a normal run. Then it might go on. Hopefully. It might not. It's up in the air to be honest. And then who knows. Hopefully someone, lots of people will like it and that means that we'll get to do it again. But with someone else in my place. I... I have to leave, you see.

MARTIN: Are you going back to Paris?

S: Yes. Briefly. Well there are already other people wanting to direct it in other countries.

MARTIN: And are you going to the other countries, too?

S: Yes. But only to see a performance or two. I'll be travelling a lot.

MARTIN: Other people are going to play me?

S: Of course. Freddie will probably continue in the part for a while. But otherwise, yes. And others will play me. And they'll change the text. They'll set it in their own countries. They'll probably have to make it make sense for their own audiences. You and I will be German or Swedish or even Japanese. And we'll speak Dutch or Portuguese instead of English.

MARTIN: But will you still speak French in the play?

S: Yes. I think that will be the only thing I insist that stays in. That and Mozart's 21st. The rest they can change.

MARTIN: It's weird.

S: What is?

MARTIN: Theatre.

S: Yes. You're right. Look. I included some photos of the show. So you can have them as a keepsake.

MARTIN: And you're sure they'll let me keep it?

S: Yes. I spoke to the governor, he's a very understanding man.

MARTIN: It must have cost a lot.

S: It's fine.

MARTIN: And you're leaving soon?

S: The day after the show closes.

MARTIN: So we won't see each other again.

S: Not this time. But I'll come visit you the next time I come back.

MARTIN: When?

S: The next time I come back to London. I'm about to film another Canadian series and you never know but it might run for a while so.

MARTIN: Will you come back?

S: Yes. I don't know. I hope so.

MARTIN: I don't have anything to give you.

S: You already gave me something very important.

MARTIN: Do you have it on you?

S: Yes. of course. I always have it on me.

MARTIN: Did you notice how your torso always smells of
jasmine afterwards?

S: Yes. Yes. It's lovely. But, are you sure you want me to have it?

MARTIN: I already gave it to you.

S: Yes. But I've been thinking it's something really important
to you.

MARTIN: That's why I gave it to you. Don't you like it?

S: Yes. Of course. How could I not like it?

MARTIN: I wanted you to have something of mine.

S: It was very important for me to have met you. I've learned
a lot.

MARTIN: We're sort of friends now.

S: Yes. Of course.

MARTIN: If you write to me… They give me the letters after.

S: I know.

MARTIN: Will you?

S: I promise. Yes, I'll send you a postcard now and again.

MARTIN: I want one of a moose. Like in the cartoons.

S: I'll send it as soon as I get to Canada.

MARTIN: Is a moose as big as it looks?

S: Bigger. They're actually huge. They're taller than this cage.

MARTIN: And have you seen a wild one.

S: Yes. Just once. In a place called Banff. But yeah. Look.
It's time. I have to go.

MARTIN: Already?

S: Yes.

MARTIN: What time is it?

S: One minute past five.

MARTIN: Can't you stay a bit longer?

S: No. It's time for me to go.

MARTIN: What do we do?

S: We embrace. Or we shake hands.

MARTIN: Alright.

S: And now we turn around and we both go home.

MARTIN: I haven't got a home.

S: Neither have I, Martin. It's a saying.

MARTIN: Saying what?

S: That we each follow our own path.

MARTIN: But I haven't got one of those, either.

S: Yes. You do.

MARTIN: A path?

S: Yes.

MARTIN: But I don't know where mine goes...

S: No one knows. I don't know, either. No one can know.

MARTIN: I'll never forget everything we talked about.

S: Neither will I. Every time I read this play or watch it on
    stage, I'll remember all our meetings.

MARTIN: The memories will persevere.

S: Yes. They will endure.

MARTIN: Come back.

S: I promise.

MARTIN: Close the door properly.

S: It's closed.

MARTIN: Otherwise the wind slams it and I don't like that.

S: Take care.

MARTIN: Safe trip.

* * *

S: I walked away without looking back. I crossed the entire
yard knowing he would be watching me leave. As soon as
I got to one of the buildings, I turned around and saw him
on the court through one of the open windows. He had sat
down and switched on his tablet. He'd chosen Mozart's
Piano Concerto N° 21 in C major. The wind carried some of
the chords of the andante to where I was standing. It was a
spring afternoon. The days were growing warmer. I stayed
a while, watching him from afar. The light from the screen
illuminated his face. Suddenly I saw his lips begin to move
slowly. Then I realised he was reading something. I've
always wondered what it might be. I never found out.

* * *

MARTIN: Citizens of Thebes. My children. New descendants
of old Cadmus. Why are you pleading before me, crowned
with supplicants' wreaths? The city is full of incense, as
well as chanting, pleas and moans, and I, because I deem
it just, not to hear it from other messengers, have come in
person, I, famous to all, I, Oedipus.

Post-script One

Please note that Martin and Freddie must ALWAYS be played by the same actor.

Post-script Two

Translator's note

Thebes Land is a work of auto-fiction. It merges true events and facts with fiction and make believe. This adaptation has, with Sergio Blanco's blessing, fictionalised elements of the real lives of the two performers cast in the production to make this adaptation live both here and now. In Sergio Blanco's original text, the character is called S as the character is a fictionalised version of Sergio who refers to real events in Sergio's life. In this adaptation, I have transferred Trevor White and Alex Austin's own lives on to the characters of S and Freddie. Martin remains untouched.

To give you a clear example of how this works in practice, in the first speech S says the following things:

That he was in On the Record at the Arcola. (True, Trevor was in On the Record at the Arcola)
That he had a drink with Mehmet in the bar (True) and pitched him two shows (False).
One of his ideas for a play was very similar to Mike Bartlett's Charles III (False)
One of his ideas for a play was the history of the Penthouse Nightclub. (False in this context. True in the sense that Trevor does want to write that play.)
That he did a Canadian TV series in Budapest and played Hotspur at the RSC (True and true)
That Mehmet called him up and told him he had a free slot. (False – Mehmet called me up and I pitched him this play.)
Etc.

A final note. In the performance of the piece itself, at the Arcola, and again with Sergio's blessing, the character S became T in order to further entrench the idea that the character was an autofictionalised version of Trevor White.

Should you wish to read the original text in Spanish, please contact Sergio directly on blancosergio71@gmail.com. Should you wish to have a chat about translating and/or autofiction with me, please feel free to contact me on daniel@casafestival.org.uk.

Daniel Goldman

Post-script Three

Translator's note. Final addendum.

In the original play, the songs used are *Amada Amante* by Roberto Carlos (in lieu of Whitney Houston) and *With or Without You* by U2 (in lieu of Foals). This was again to make the piece live here and now for a UK audience.

WWW.OBERONBOOKS.COM

Follow us on www.twitter.com/@oberonbooks
& www.facebook.com/OberonBooksLondon